FINDING *Sarah,* FINDING *Me*

FINDING *Sarah,* FINDING *Me*

A Birth Mother's Story

CHRISTINE LINDSAY

WhiteFire Publishing

FINDING SARAH, FINDING ME

WhiteFire Publishing
13607 Bedford Rd NE
Cumberland, MD 21502

ISBN: 978-1-939023-82-7 (digital)
978-1-939023-81-0 (print)

Other Titles by Christine Lindsay

FICTION

Historical Trilogy Twilight of the British Raj

Book 1 *Shadowed in Silk*

Book 2 *Captured by Moonlight*

Book 3 *Veiled at Midnight*

Londonderry Dreaming

Heavenly Haven (short Christmas story)

Sofi's Bridge

NON-FICTION

Finding Sarah, Finding Me

Go to www.ChristineLindsay.org

for more about author Christine Lindsay

and to sign up for her quarterly newsletter on new releases.

Introduction

by William Blaney,
Executive Director of Global Aid Network.

I have been told that one in three people's lives have been touched by adoption. That would certainly be true for our family. Our lives have been so blessed by our daughter-in-law Sarah, who was adopted and is part of the journey shared in *Finding Sarah, Finding Me.* Sarah and my son Mark are the parents of two of our grandchildren. You see, these precious grandchildren would not have been possible had Christine decided to abort Sarah. Sarah's positive impact on so many lives through her love and devotion to God and people would have been lost, and that would have been a tragedy.

As Executive Director of Global Aid Network (GAiN) Canada, I greatly value Sarah and Mark's passion to relieve suffering and to practically demonstrate God's love, in word and deed, to hurting and needy people around the world. Their chosen profession as registered nurses allows them to touch the lives of so many people. As of the writing of this book, Sarah is on maternity leave from her job as Project Manager for GAiN's Women's and Children's programs, which focus primarily on working with orphans and fatherless children.

My wife Susan and I have known about Sarah's adoption story since shortly after she and Mark began dating as teenagers. We fell in love with Sarah. It was just before Sarah and Mark were married that Christine reached out to Hans and Anne, Sarah's adoptive parents, to see if they would allow Sarah and Christine to meet. This book chronicles this journey. It is a journey with many peaks and valleys, of great joy and fulfilled hope. It is a complex journey, but one that has touched the lives of so many people. For life is God's gift to us. Decisions we make will impact our life's journey, and sometimes these outcomes appear to be all but hopeless. But joy awaits those who stay the course. *Finding Sarah, Finding Me* chronicles two lives and decisions made that resulted in incredible joy in this journey we call life.

Being adopted has not solely defined Sarah. Her adoption story, rather, is only one facet of her life. As you read *Finding Sarah, Finding Me*, you will see that adoption does not solely define Christine either, or Anne and Hans, Sarah's adoptive parents. Their story is really about God's ever-guiding hand on each of their lives to achieve His purposes. It is, in the truest sense, a love story. We serve an amazing God who actually uses you and me—who make poor decisions, are weak, broken, and hurting—to touch the lives of so many people. Our lives are a testimony to others walking the same journey, for God brings light in the midst of our darkness, hope in our hopelessness.

I feel privileged to be part of Sarah and Christine's story, and to offer my thoughts on this work. Christine, having become aware of the work of GAiN through Sarah, has shared with me that she could not accept payment for this story that is so precious to her. In the serendipitous manner that God worked in her story of finding her birth-daughter Sarah and thereby herself, Christine has arranged for 100% of author royalties to be donated to the Women and Children's Initiative with GAiN. These royalties will be used to bring hope and joy to the women and children we are privileged to touch with Christ's love, thus bringing these lives into God's story for Sarah and Christine. I know that you will be deeply touched by this love story. If you know someone who is on a similar journey, please share this book with them. For God uses each of our stories in His great redemptive story, to bring hope and a new day to those He has brought into our lives for that purpose.

This book is dedicated to my mother,
Sarah Martha Caroline Lindsay,
who taught me that I was only on loan to her for a while,
that I really belonged to God.
Through her maternal love I learned about
the depths of love in the heart of...
Our Father who art in heaven.

NOTE TO READER

The following is the compiling and weaving of five different adoption reunions. As the main author, I have designated each reunion in reference to the following adoptees:

- Anna in Oregon
- Cathy in Bermuda
- Levi in Manitoba, Canada
- Sarah in the Fraser Valley, Canada
- Susan in South Africa

As members from all sides of the adoption triad, we acknowledge that adoption and adoption reunions are as different as the people in this world. Adoption is born out of loss, and while not all adoptions are happy, many are. We share our stories here for one reason only: to encourage and inspire you in whatever heartache you are experiencing, whether it pertains to adoption or not.

Each chapter (except for the last) opens with a part of my story as I begin the search for my birth-daughter Sarah, up to and after our reunion to present day. In the second segment of each chapter, I share memories of my pregnancy, delivering Sarah, relinquishing her, and after the relinquishment leading up to my search for her. Each chapter ends with a vignette from a person from one of the other adoption stories, showing his or her unique perspective.

It is my deepest prayer that through this story you will see the face of the heavenly Father, that you will feel him lifting up your chin and grow warm in his smile.

Foreword

In the years between, after relinquishing Sarah at three days old and before our reunion many years later, if I just happen to attend a women's conference or a ladies' church function around her birthday, and as happens so often, the organizers of the event just happen to hand out carnations at the door...and as they randomly give out a variety of colors to the ladies leaving...as I inch my way slowly toward the exit in a long lineup of women, I watch with mounting expectation.

The flowers arrive every year around her birthday, those silly blooms that started on the day I got out of the hospital. Sometimes just a card with flowers on it, and always from someone who has no clue what February 24th means to me. Sometimes a friend might send a potted plant—always pink—just because they're thinking of me.

So as I shuffle forward in each lineup at any ladies' function I happen to attend, while the last strains of the last song float over the venue, and as the women in front of me smile and with thanks receive their red carnation—or yellow or white—as a gift for coming, without ever asking, mine is always, always pink.

I lift my bloom to my face and breathe in the sweetness. *Yes, Lord, you want me to find Sarah.*

1

Do Not Be Afraid

Christine, February 1999

Two months before the reunion

The clandestine nature of my trip paints a picture of me I don't want to look at too closely. As I drive from Maple Ridge to Abbotsford twenty miles away, I wonder if I am one heartbeat away from being a stalker.

I find the high school after several wrong turns. Squelching down the fear of getting caught, I park in the school lot and drum up the nerve to walk in the front doors. I repeat under my breath, "It's no different than walking into Lana's high school at home in Maple Ridge. It's no different at all."

I'm an ordinary person just like any ordinary parent in the Fraser Valley, the Bible Belt of British Columbia. I'm a Sunday school teacher, a bonded bank teller, a woman of forty-one, hair lightened blond, dressed like any nice mom in jeans, casual shirt, running shoes, my bag slung over my shoulder. I am David's wife, mom to seventeen-year-old Lana, fifteen-year-old Kyle, and ten-year-old Robert.

I am also the woman who wrote in her journal last night, "For twenty years I've comforted myself that this time would come, that my birth-daughter and I could legally be reunited. And now I am afraid of her."

I, I, I, yes *I* am all of the above. I hate my self-centered focus. Am I also obsessive? And dear God—am I stalking my firstborn?

There's still time to turn around, get back in my car, forget this whole crazy escapade. Instead, coldness grips my spine as I stride past the office, praying none of the staff will stop me and ask why I'm here, like a criminal.

I'm only coming to Sarah's former school just this once, not driving past her house like a real stalker, although I have the address. At least I've held myself back from that temptation. This one look—in a public place—I'll allow myself. But I shudder.

Who can understand my hunger to know, to see? My husband and my mother understand, but do I deserve their pity? Close friends can relate yet aren't able to hold back their trepidation. Those in any adoption triad who search for that missing biological connection will understand. I've heard plenty of their wild stories at the adoption support group. Certainly the militant ones with agendas of their own, if they knew what I was up to today, would urge me to barge forward despite my qualms. The average person though? Would they understand this slipping over the edge into a gray area that frightens the daylights out of me?

But time now stops. Not far from the office I find what I'm looking for. This moment I've awaited for twenty years. A hectic school hall with teenagers rushing to their next class drifts away. Bell sounds recede to a muffled hush. A desperate quiet roars in my head. It's the same in every school—a wall displays mounted photos of each graduating class. Portraits of each graduate. Being this close to something tangible emphasizes the growing fragility I've battled the past two years. My soul stretches paper-thin as I search the pictures. They're easy enough to follow, in alphabetical order, and I search for students' names starting with the letter V.

I've waited so long. Far longer than I ever anticipated the search to be. Disappointment after disappointment, lost letters, lost files, that awful sense of being forgotten. The past few weeks as her twentieth birthday looms, my emotional pain has built to a mushroom cloud. I hardly recognize myself anymore.

And then there it is. *Sarah VandenBos.* Her grad picture. Her face.

A wall of air slams into the core of my being, pushing me backward. It's hard to catch my breath, and I freeze. After all these years of Sarah being a shadowy picture in my imagination, at last I see her features.

Her long hair falls slightly wavy in that dark blond shade, the exact color as mine at her age. Her eyes hold something of me too, the shape of her head, her neck showing above her grad gown, even something about her teeth. For a moment, my own college graduation picture superimposes itself over Sarah's. A ghost from the past, what I looked like shortly before I became pregnant with her. Yet there's something else in Sarah's face, something I didn't expect, though I should have.

Her birth father Jim surfaces through her features too. Her mouth is the same shape as his, her nose has that crazy blending of parental genes. Thank God she's got the tip of my nose and the bridge of Jim's and not the other way around. For the past twenty years I've imagined her as a younger version of me, but now seeing the real Sarah, flesh and blood and no longer a phantom of my imagination, the foundation of my life rumbles and shifts.

As I study every visible facet of her face, a few more pencil lines in the mental portrait of me are erased. She's beautiful, just as I've always imagined...as beautiful as Lana. And there's such confidence in Sarah's smile. Sure, this is a professional grad photo and is supposed to exude that balance of poise and assurance, but even while my pride in her and thankfulness soar, I want to shrink away and hide. There's nothing lacking in this lovely face, nothing to show there's even an ounce of need. This is what a young woman looks like whose cup of love has been filled to the brim.

How could such a girl ever need me? Sarah isn't the needy one. I am. I'm the one who hurts because I am not her mother.

I've stood staring at the grad photos long enough. No one seems to notice me, but I have no right to be here, and it's time to go. On the drive home I grip the steering wheel. Tears slide down to soak my shirt collar. Now that I've seen her, my fears of meeting her escalate. She has her own life, her own family. At the same time, every atom in my body continues to shove me forward, to keep hoping for the eventual relationship with Sarah that I crave. These constant extremes of emotion drain the life out of me, and I want to just run away, disappear.

A particular psalm has given me strange comfort these past months. "I lie down and sleep; I wake again, because the Lord sustains me," resonates within me. But it's not the poetic phrases of King David in Psalm three that bring comfort—rather, the facts surrounding the psalmist's situation soothe like a salve on a raw wound. The psalmist wrote those words as he looked back on the time he fled from his son Absalom.

Certainly Absalom was one wicked man out to murder his father and steal the throne. Those melodramatic circumstances are vastly different from my search for my birth-daughter, a nice ordinary girl in the Fraser Valley. But sensational tabloid accounts of messy lives fill the Bible and give me this peculiar peace.

At this moment, driving home with my emotions rocking off their base, I'm consoled by King David's stewing in a similar emotional quagmire. He too loved his child, wanted his child with all his heart, yet ran to mountain caves to cower from his own flesh and blood. I'm not proud of my feelings, but they spill out in a bitter stream from my journals each night. December 29, 1998—"I look back now, and for my sake wish I had not given Sarah up. She is my flesh and blood, yet she loves another couple as her parents. I struggle day and night about meeting her. Why do I torture myself with this compulsion to be reunited?"

Terrible words to flow from a mother's heart. What kind of a mother am I? A mother to only three of her children, but not to her firstborn. A fractured mother. In spite of this, my husband and I are happily married, a happiness attained by hard work and moving past our failures with forgiveness. Our three kids are our unmitigated joy. Yet I hunger for Sarah, whom I search for. And fear.

It was all so different from twenty years earlier. At seven months pregnant, I'd written in my journal in 1979 my longings that the pregnancy would never end. During those last four months I'd not wanted the day to come that I'd arranged to give up my baby. Heavy with child then, I'd layered the relinquishment of my little one with as much peace and love as I layered the layette—of soft undershirts, fluffy sleepers, the little white Bible—all to be given to her adoptive parents so that they and Sarah would know how deeply I loved her, how much I wanted to see her again one day.

I had the strength to do all that back then because I was sure God had promised me a special relationship for Sarah and me when she was grown. So I'd given Sarah up in 1979, banking on that promise. God simply couldn't let me down.

But then, King David had banked on God too, only to have his heart broken by his child.

Remembering back to June, 1978

Jim and I watched the movie *The Goodbye Girl* on one of our first dates. With just a hint of the drama queen that sadly still surfaces in me, I remember thinking, *Yeah that's me, the goodbye girl.* I counted up my goodbyes—at five years old to my entire extended family in Ireland when we immigrated to Canada. At twelve, my goodbye to my father when my parents divorced. At nineteen, goodbye to all my old friends in Ontario when my mother, sister, and little brother and I ran away to start over again in British Columbia. And now a year later, the goodbye I'd just said to Jim a few weeks ago when he went up north to work on an oilrig. I missed him.

I thought about Jim as I sat at my desk in the little island of reception in the Woodward's China Buying Office, my first full-time job. I wondered if we had a chance as a couple. If our going together would ever amount to marriage. Still, while the heat outside blanketed Vancouver, I worried more about what was happening inside me.

I missed my period—so what? But I knew. *Miss-Regular-as-Clockwork does not miss her period.*

Half the staff left the office, walking past glass cases filled with Waterford crystal and English bone china. Their laughter dwindled as they rose as a gaggle up the escalator, heading for the cafeteria. The main extension rang, and I answered.

With hardly any preamble, the clinical voice on the other end said, "Miss Lindsay, your pregnancy test has returned positive."

My mouth went dry, and I no longer heard the clacking of calculators but of blood whooshing through my temple. Positive? Negative?

With the naiveté of a twenty-year-old, I asked, "Does this mean I'm going to have a baby?"

"Yes."

Deep inside me, the tinkling sound of breaking crystal. Everything receded, including the voice of the doctor's receptionist.

I hung up the phone and swayed forward on my chair. Below me lay the beige linoleum tiles of the floor. *Oh, God, let me fall through the floor. Let it swallow me up. Let me be invisible.* Unmarried pregnancies didn't happen to nice Christian girls. But then, I wasn't a nice Christian. I was a lousy Christian.

The other office girls must have returned from their coffee break. The work day must have ended. Somehow, I boarded a bus. Blinded by tears, I sat on the aisle seat, halfway down, and stared at the dirty floor beneath my feet. I was pregnant. No husband. Jim circled in and out of my life like a revolving door. What good could Jim do anyway? Would he clean up his life, give up the drugs? Would he suddenly become a responsible adult and marry me? Take care of this...this tiny thing growing inside me?

I swallowed through a tight throat. I would not cry, at least not until I was alone. But before I went home to my empty, single apartment, I needed my mother. At the very least, there was always Mum.

I got off the bus close to her place. When she opened the door, with one glance at me her chin shifted upward. Her eyes darkened with worry. She put an arm around my shoulders and led me inside. "What's wrong?"

The words tumbled out. "I'm pregnant."

I wasn't afraid to tell her, but I hated to. My world had shattered. As her eldest child, the one who had always done well at school, gone to college, she and I had planned a different life for me. A better life waited for me out there, with a satisfying career, someday a devoted husband, and a home. Not the vicious cycle of single-motherhood and poverty.

She held me.

There wasn't much else to say. She knew about Jim, and from her own life she knew the story well. A foolish girl takes the risk of unprotected sex with a guy whose love is for something other than her. In my mother's case, my father loved alcohol. As for me, my competition for Jim's love was a bag of weed or a white line of cocaine.

My mother sat with me on the couch, her arms around me, and together we cried. "Don't worry," she said. "We'll get through this together."

My mum, sister, little brother, and I had learned long ago to be a tight unit. After talking for a while, being with Mum gave me the strength to go home. A soft summer evening tried to cradle me as I walked the two miles to my own apartment. I'd taken such pride in decorating my little place, my first stride toward independence, and I'd blown it. I'd probably conceived my baby within these walls. I shut the door behind me. Dropping my purse at the open balcony window, I took in the bachelor suite. So quiet. Loneliness closed in around me, and I slumped to my knees.

All the while I'd been with my mother, though I'd cried with her, wiped hot tears from my face, I'd been able to hold back the torrent. Now the volatile storm gathered, rising up inside me in heaps. My mouth spread wide in silent sobs, my arms clutched my stomach, and I bent over, my head swaying back and forth only inches from the carpet. *This can't be true. This can't be true.*

But it was. How could I have been such a fool? At twenty years old I should have known better. Even though I loved Jim, in my heart I referred to him as my walk-on-the-wild-side. The skim-milk love he had for me wouldn't be enough now that I was going to have his baby.

I wrapped my arms around my middle and rocked on my knees, bawling until nothing remained. My face stung with drying salt, and my hand crept to my abdomen.

Deep inside me slept a tiny bit of flesh. At eight weeks, how big or small did this scrap of humanity measure? Did its heart beat? I'd seen pictures of fetuses in the womb, sucking their thumbs. Did mine have a face yet, a spine? If I left it alone to grow, how soon would it become a boy or a girl? *But I'm so scared, dear God, I'm so scared.*

Twilight snuffed out the last of the day, and I tried to remember what I knew about God. I knew his Son from Sunday school—a gentle, kind man in a white robe, his feet covered in dust, who I'd been told didn't shoo people away when they'd blown it, especially tainted women, like I was now.

But God? The heavenly Father? What on earth did a father's love feel like? Who needed a father anyway?

One of the clearest memories of my dad stole back into my mind, a memory I'd tried to bury over the years. But the memory kept slinking back like a mangy cat steals under the porch no matter how many times you scare it away. As a child of seven and in the hospital for pneumonia, I'd waited for my dad. It was his evening to visit, and my mother had made that possible by staying home with my sister. From my hospital bed I peered out the window to the street below, looking for his figure to walk up the pavement.

Daddy never showed up. Ten minutes after visiting hours ended, he sheepishly staggered in. A frowning nurse allowed him five minutes with me. The beer on his breath wafted over me as he leaned over to kiss my forehead. How rarely he kissed me. Nonetheless, his smelly kiss filled the cold emptiness that had bunched up in my chest as I'd waited for him. When he left me minutes later, even as a kid of seven, I knew my dad spent the time he should have been visiting me down at the pub. I also knew he was on his way back to the pub to order another beer.

The only parental love I'd known came from my mother. Now at twenty I was going to be a mother. Maybe God would be there for me as my mum had always been.

Did God's voice echo in my own when I protectively wrapped my arms around my abdomen and said, "I love you, little one. I'll take care of you. Don't be afraid."?

From Oregon, USA—The Adoption of Anna
"Trying to Imagine My Daughter's Reunion with Her Birth Parents"
by adoptive father David Sanford

I wept hard the day my wife, Renée, and I formally asked if we could adopt our youngest daughter, Anna. We wept in response to reading a two-inch high stack of police reports, medical records, evaluations, and other official documents describing the hell Anna endured during the first three years of her life.

That spring Renée and I received the great news that we were approved to adopt Anna. When we went to her foster home, she jumped into our arms and said, "It's my family!" A week later she moved to our home. That evening she and our youngest son, Benjamin, spontaneously started dancing to the music playing in the background. An hour later they were still dancing. Our hearts overflowed with gratitude and love.

I could write a book telling story after story about why I love, cherish, and adore Anna. Then again, as we knew would be the case, the nightmares of her past came back to haunt her and us during her early adolescence. Three stories stand out as particularly poignant and apropos.

Shortly after Thanksgiving, a few weeks before her fifteenth birthday, Anna told me she had a secret. She then proceeded to tell me about a lullaby she has sung to herself every night since we adopted her. I asked her to write down the simple lyrics, which appear below. Anna was clear: "These lyrics are how I sing it, not necessarily what my birth dad and mom sang to me." The lyrics could echo Randy Newman's song "Sandman's Coming" sung by Linda Ronstadt (and others). In any case, I designed a poster for Anna with a dark blue sky, moon, and stars in the background and the lyrics of Anna's lullaby in bold black letters.

> Sleep our little baby,
> Sleep our little girl,
> Mommy and Daddy love you,
> Sleep our little baby, sleep.

Some days later Anna was all smiles as I took her on a date to a nice restaurant. I explained to her that two of our goals that evening were to have fun and make sure we got to know our server by name and make it a fun evening for him too. Anna loved the idea, and we had a delightful time talking, teasing our server, and talking some more.

At one point Anna brought up her nightmares about her birth

father. I looked down. In a low voice I wondered aloud if he was still alive. Unbeknownst to me, Anna misunderstood my demeanor and statement. The next morning when she talked it over with Renée, Anna said I wished her birth father were dead. Renée immediately corrected her, saying I would never say something like that, to Anna's great relief.

That previous evening Anna also brought up her birth mother. I surprised her by saying that a couple of years earlier Renée had found a photo of her birth mom on Facebook. As promised, I looked through our archives and found the photo Renée had downloaded and printed. Sadly, the photo "backfired" almost immediately. Anna had already been acting out, but her behavior became much worse, including shallow but extensive cuttings up and down her wrist. As well, Anna's nightmares about her birth father got worse.

In English class shortly after New Year's, Anna and her classmates were asked to write a poem in class. After a few minutes Anna stopped writing and sat at her desk in a reflective mood. Her teacher walked over and asked if Anna was still trying to get an idea for her poem. Anna handed a page to her.

After reading the page, Anna's teacher asked who wrote it.

"I did," Anna replied.

"But it's been only a few minutes."

"I know. The poem came to me very quickly."

"This sounds like an older, more experienced writer."

Anna wasn't sure what to say next. "Our poems aren't due for a few days, so I may work on mine a bit more."

That evening Anna and I read through her poem several times. An idea came to her, and she quickly typed three more lines about "my shredded paper heart." With her permission, I've reprinted the finished poem below.

Who Am I?

Who am I? Who are you?
Me Daughter. You Father.
Father? Yes Father.
That's who you are.
I know you, but
you do not know me.
Sweat, blood, anger, fear,
they're all one to me,
one person. But who?
Let me tell you...
The sweat is from nightmares that haunt me still today,
but these nightmares are memories,
memories of you Father.
Blood is what came from the gash in my head,
the one you gave me Father, remember?
Blood from the cut on my heart,
my shredded paper heart, for
I have been torn apart by your words.
Anger is the gnashing of teeth,
the hate that triples every time your hand hit my side.
Fear is still tied to my past,
the fear of not letting go.
The fear that you're still here.
Who am I? Who are you?
I know who I am, but
I don't know you.

~ Annalise C. Sanford

As you undoubtedly have guessed, trying to imagine Anna's reunion with her birth father is almost impossible apart from a miracle of God.

Then again, could arrangements be made for Anna to meet her birth mom sometime in the next few years? Yes, though Renée and I know it could "backfire" and send Anna spiraling seemingly out of control for weeks, maybe months.

After all, what could that woman possibly say to Anna's desperate questions: "How could you abandon me as a baby? How could you leave me with that man? Do you have any idea how badly I was abused emotionally, physically, and sexually the next couple of years? Why did you flee without me?"

What does the future hold for Anna? Much sorrow and much good. This evening I told Anna how I deeply wished I could erase all the horror of her first years of life. She looked at me and replied, "But Dad, if you could do that, how would I ever be able to help others?"

Who knows? God still makes trophies of grace. Anna certainly is one. We pray that God uses her to win her birth mother's heart. We also pray for the conversion of her birth father and his reconciliation with the precious young woman that Anna is becoming.

David Sanford's writings have been published everywhere from Focus on the Family to Forbes. His book and Bible projects have been published by Doubleday, Thomas Nelson, Tyndale, and Zondervan. His speaking engagements have ranged everywhere from The Billy Graham Center at the Cove to the University of California Berkeley. His professional biography is summarized at http://www.linkedin.com/in/drsanford. His personal biography features his wife of 34 years, Renée, their five children, and their 11 grandchildren (including one in heaven).

2

He Sees Me

Christine, spring 1997

Two years before the reunion, at the start of the search

Just as I've done for the past eighteen years, I lift down the box from the back of my closet, feeling all the stealth of a Cold War spy. The box might as well be marked TOP SECRET. Few people know of the contents: my journals from my pregnancy with Sarah, the two hospital ID bracelets, mine and the tiny one that clasped around her baby ankle, and fragments of dried pink flower petals almost gray with the passage of time. Clues to that secret me, mother of a secret child.

My husband, David, has known about my firstborn from the night of our engagement. So do my mother, my sister, Irene, and a few friends who've been sworn to secrecy. And of course, my younger brother, Stephen, knew once my sister let the cat out of the bag when he was a teenager. But I kept the knowledge of my oldest daughter limited to a select few. That's the way things are done—or, at least, used to be.

Secrecy—how many families are tied together with the sticky tape of concealment? But quietly, year after year, I keep the truth even from my own kids. Every once in a while I savor the contents of the box and afterward replace it in the closet and go about my life.

Typical boys, Kyle and Robert are never interested in sappy movies about adoption reunions. So whenever those movies come on TV, it's usually only Lana and I who curl up on the couch to watch them. Violin music swells as the moment slides closer and closer to when the birth mother and child—and often other siblings—meet for the first time. Lana's gaze is always glued to the screen during those scenes while my gaze never leaves her face. *This* is my little girl. Sarah's adoptive mom has Sarah, and I have Lana.

I silently delight in the daughter God allowed me to keep and pray that Lana will understand one day when I tell her about her sister. The secret is hardest to keep from her. Ever since Lana was a little girl, she's told me she wants a big sister—not a little sister like most girls ask for—as though God scooped out a place in her heart for Sarah all along. But as I start my search I'm more worried about my sons. How will Kyle and Robert react when David and I tell them about Sarah?

I turn back to watch the happy-ever-after ending of the TV drama, everyone wiping away tears of joy, and reassure myself. My reunion with Sarah is going to be even better than this TV version because God himself is directing our production.

As of the start of 1997, Lana and Kyle are in high school and Robert is still our little boy. David and the kids are everything to me. The harsh edges to the pain of giving up Sarah have gentled over the years to an ache only remembered once a day when I pray for her and her parents. Sarah belongs to that couple who remain in the shadows, unknown to me. I've accepted that. I've done my homework on adoption. They are her parents. I am her birth mother. My role is her distant guiding star while her mom and dad are the sun in her orbit. I know my role and rejoice in the marvelous things God does through adoption.

Or so I keep telling myself.

Ever since the day I relinquished Sarah in 1979, I've wanted to meet her parents. All through the years of Sarah's growing up I imagined a reunion that includes them. With a lack of sophistication, I admit, I envision Sarah's family and ours like long-lost relatives, all sitting around the table, passing roast beef, mashed potatoes, and smiling at finally being together.

As my imagination gallops, at the back of my mind I keep pulling on the reins. *Use some common sense*, I tell myself. *If your fear of rejection shakes you awake in the middle of the night, how are Sarah's parents going to feel when you ask for a relationship with their child?*

But I close my ears to my worries. Nope, God gave me the impression all those years ago that he would reserve a special relationship for Sarah and me, and that includes her parents. I cling to my vision that Sarah, her mom, and I are going to be the poster girls for adoption. Together we'll stand up in churches and encourage others in the adoption triad. As the birth mom, I'll reassure pregnant girls to take this leap of faith, trusting there is the reward of reunion at the end of their loss. A Christian either acts in faith or they don't.

But the words of Oswald Chambers in the devotional book *My Utmost for His Highest* tap me on the shoulder. "Faith in antagonism to common sense is fanaticism, and common sense in antagonism to faith is rationalization. The life of faith brings the two into a right relation."

So am I following romantic impulses stimulated by TV? Or am I being led by heavenly inspiration? For the past few weeks after her eighteenth birthday, I've gone to the phone and started to call the counselor who'd arranged the private adoption eighteen years ago.

Bob Trainor worked through a Christian counseling service called Burden Bearers, and I still had his number. If anyone can find Sarah and her parents, Bob can. In a year's time Sarah will reach her age of majority, and we can legally be reunited. But each time I start dialing Bob's number, I replace the receiver before my call connects.

What right have I to search for Sarah? She's happy. I just know that in my bones. She or her parents might be hurt by my intrusion.

Still, a month after her birthday, with the contents of my secret box on my lap, I phone Bob. He calls back that very night, and a few days later I enter his office. I haven't seen Bob since David and I got married.

As I shake his hand, the now white-haired Bob is full of enthusiasm to help me locate Sarah and her parents, but his brow wrinkles as he leans back in his office chair. He no longer works for Burden Bearers but has his own practice. He's certain he can dig through his personal files and find Sarah's parents' names and address. "In the meantime, write a letter to Sarah," he says. "I'll deliver it."

"What about my kids? When should I tell them?"

Bob advises me to not tell the boys about Sarah until we hear that she actually wants to meet me, but he agrees it's time to share the truth with Lana.

My mind rockets like July's fireworks as I speed the thirty miles from Bob's office to my hometown. It's really going to happen. I'm going to find Sarah. Finally, this chafing secrecy between Lana and me is going to end. That afternoon, in a whirl of shopping, I find the perfect journal with pink and blue hydrangeas on the front cover and race home from the mall to start writing my letter.

After making dinner for David and the kids and washing the dishes quickly with a promise to do a better job next time around, I put pen to paper and start to draft a letter. "I'll be honest with you, Sarah, right now I have a lot of different emotions running through me. I'm nervous, unsure of myself, yet terribly excited just to be writing to you at long last. There's fear, faith, and there's sadness too, but also a lot of joy."

And a little later in the first of many drafts I write, "Sarah, I want to tell you about your sister. Lana has always been a quiet person, but these last few years, as she nears graduation, she's developed a very dry sense of humor. She's sweet and funny and really tough on her two younger brothers."

I lift my pen from the page and smile. *Lana—at long last I can tell Lana.*

David and I arrange to take Lana out to lunch alone after church the very next Sunday. We wait for her in the car. As usual, she's dillydallying in the church library hunting for a book.

"So, how are we going to break this to her?" I ask David. I've only been visualizing telling Lana about her sister since the days I cuddled her as a baby. "I could start by—"

"I'll do it." David focuses his gaze at the front of the car, his hands gripping the steering wheel.

I look through the windshield at the now empty church parking lot and sigh. "Okay, but I think you should start by saying—"

"Honey, let me break it to her. I've been thinking about this day for a long time too." My husband casts me a look that conveys all the years he's quietly celebrated Sarah's birthday with me.

I sink back on an exhale. "Okay, okay." I can hardly wait for it to happen, and yet...no. Is Lana really going to be okay with this? This huge rearrangement of the planets in our family orbit?

Our heads turn to watch Lana run out of the church, waving a book in her hands. "Mom, Mom, look at this cool book I got."

Lana slips into the backseat and slams the door. She hands a book to me. *The Shunning* by Beverly Lewis. "See, Mom, it's about this Amish girl who goes up to the attic and finds this old trunk and discovers she's really adopted, and then she goes out and looks for her birth mom." She barely stops for breath.

Sensations of floating in outer space wash over me. Here I am in my spacesuit, whirling, twirling against a star-filled sky. *Of all the novels for Lana to grab hold of today.* Somewhat giddy, I look blindly out the window as David drives to the mall on this bright day in early spring. I slant a glance at my husband, who struggles to control his grin. Lana reaches over the front seat and takes her book back from me to begin reading.

When we reach the A&W, David runs his hand across my shoulders and gives me a sideways hug before we go inside. After we eat our burgers and sip the rest of our soda, David clears his throat. On the outside I probably look normal while on the inside I continue floating in outer space.

"Honey," David says to Lana with just the slightest hitch in his cadence. "That's a really interesting book you're reading. Are any—" He clears his throat again. "Are any of your friends adopted? Do you know much about adoption?"

Lana lifts her gaze, now laden with concern, from her book to stare into her father's eyes—eyes the exact same shade of blue as her own under her fringe of long brunette hair. She sends a puzzled look to me, then back to her dad. "Are you trying to tell me I'm adopted?"

I close my eyes. *Way to go, David.* But a wave of joy carries me along, weightless. Just like I've always known, and like her full name means, Lana Joy was going to be okay with this.

David pulls himself up straight, his expression blank. "No! You're not adopted." He sends me a watered-downed smile and starts again.

"You've been ours from day one. It's that Mom, well...your mom gave a child up for adoption before she and I met and got married. A little girl."

Lana listens intently to the rest of the story, flicking glances at me. Then she does exactly what I've always thought she'd do. She looks away to process the revelation and then turns her blue gaze on me, her cautious look changing to awe. "I've got a sister?" It amazes me how few questions Lana has. All she wants to know is about this baby girl—her sister—who's grown up apart from her in another family. The sparkle in Lana's voice dances in her eyes.

If I could see my life from beginning to end, I know this moment is one of its happiest. I sit back, letting wholeness seep through me. My feet find solid ground. Now my daughter can start to see the real me.

Remembering back to June, 1978

A few weeks after the doctor confirmed my pregnancy, Jim stood at my door. He'd come down from his work on the oilrig. He pulled me close, and I breathed in the clean soapy scent of him. My tears wet his plaid flannel shirt that smelled faintly of ordinary tobacco, but not of the cloying odor of marijuana. *Oh, please God, help him love me and the baby enough.*

We moved to sit on my sofa. His eyes were clear, his pupils normal and not pinpoints shying away from light. He was sober, but for how long? My hopes jangled like a crazy marionette on strings as Jim hugged me close. I loved him, didn't I? True, I believed in God and Jim didn't. But I could set aside a lot if Jim would care enough about our baby and me to give up his drugs.

Leaning my head on his shoulder, I knew that if he asked me to marry him, I'd say yes and hope for the best. Thousands of people got married on the same premise every year.

His smile trembled as he stood and gestured helplessly, looking at the ceiling, the walls, the world outside the window, anywhere but at me. "I don't know what to say, Chris...."

"How do you feel about the baby?" I asked with a hollow voice. *That little person growing inside of me that might have your smile or my eyes?*

He shrugged, his eyes pleading with me to understand. "It doesn't feel like...it...has anything to do with me."

It doesn't feel like it has anything to do with him? Our child was not an "it." I walked away from him to the kitchen.

He followed. "You and I are just getting started." He shrugged again. "I'm not ready...for this."

I'd known before we started talking that I was the only one willing to take on the role of parent, but Jim's words cut the strings. I rested my forehead against the cool fridge door as my jangling marionette of hope crashed to the floor. I'd been hoping for too big a miracle. Jim wasn't going to change overnight, and with his dependence on marijuana and alcohol, could I really trust him to make the best decisions for anyone, even himself? My own life had been filled with a string of disappointments from my dad. This pale, fledgling love Jim and I had for each other would never be enough.

I pushed away from the fridge. No way would I let my baby have the same kind of childhood that I'd had.

Before Jim returned to the oilrig up north, he and I drove the short distance to his parents' place. I suppose I went with one last crazy hope that something could be salvaged from our relationship.

Maybe his parents would help.

Their home was everything I'd wanted since I was a kid. Middle-class split-level, quality teak furniture without being showy. Classy, comfortable, not a collection of hand-me-downs like the homes my mother had done her best to provide. Jim's parents had been secure in their marriage and finances, and they had not only raised the child who had been born to them but had adopted Jim as well.

The furrows in their brows told me clearly that Jim's mom and dad had not expected me that evening. At first their anger zeroed in on Jim as we all perched on the edges of sofas and chairs. "Jimmy, how could you have been so stupid?" As the conversation went on, their strained voices targeted both Jim and me. "It would be the height of foolishness for the two of you to try and raise a baby."

It didn't take long before Jim's parents, their mouths and eyes rigid, flung questions—red hot pokers just out of the fire—toward me alone. "Why didn't you use birth control? Have you considered all options? You don't have to have this baby. There are other ways."

Jim at least winced for me. He'd hinted at abortion earlier on the way to his parents' place. For a long time I'd struggled with my Christian faith, especially now with fear climbing my spine. How could I bring this baby into the world by myself? But I'd always wonder—a boy? A girl? Would I ever be able to forget? Handle that kind of loss?

Anger crouched inside me, ready to leap in defense of my baby. With their comfortable living standards, this was all Jim's parents could suggest? At least their anger combined with my own stiffened my backbone, enabling me to walk out of their shipshape, middle-class house with Jim. With a helpless shrug, he drove me back to my apartment and left for his job in the north. My two-room bachelorette suite echoed with silence, but I preferred this silence.

Anger no longer crouched inside me—it leapt and began to bound. Here in this lonely little apartment with God's help, I had to buck up. *Get strong. Fight like a tiger for your baby. Make the hard choices. You're a mother now.*

I flicked on the lamp, sat on the couch, and grabbed my Bible, flipping through it, searching for what I'd read a few days earlier. That story that had given me strength. Where was it? I needed something to help me go through this pregnancy by myself. I found the story in the book of Genesis, about a woman called Hagar. Through a complicated set of circumstances, Hagar's master, Abraham, impregnated her. Abraham and his wife, Sarah, had their own self-centered reasons for letting this happen, but for Hagar it boiled down to eventual banishment both for her and her unborn child. Boy did I know how that felt.

Under a blistering sky, quivering white with heat, Hagar ran and fell to the desert floor. But God followed her out to that arid, empty place and made promises to care for her and her child, to protect them, to give this small family of two a future.

Leaning on her hands and knees in the sand, Hagar screamed out to God. "You see me, don't you? Yes! You see me."

She choked on an indrawn breath. "And now I see you."

It didn't matter to me that this story in Genesis focused on Abraham as the chosen one to father Israel. All that mattered to me as I cried over my Bible was that God had seen a poor, unwanted, pregnant woman like me, and he cared.

I wanted to trust God for me and my baby. He wasn't like my earthly dad, was he, when I was in hospital and he got drunk down at the pub?

God, you see me, don't you? Please tell me you won't let me down.

From Bermuda—the Adoption of Cathy
"You Don't Know Me"
by author and adoptee Cathy West

There was a time I thought I didn't need to know the truth about where I came from.

Until one day I did.

It was an overpowering sense of need, a keening, really, to find answers to the questions I'd secretly been asking all my life. Questions that used to frighten me and stir up confusion and feelings I didn't know what to do with. Questions I felt guilty for wanting answers to.

Now in my thirties with two children, I had to find the courage to start asking. I also needed to accept that I might not get any answers. Or the ones I wanted.

It's said that some adoptees often fantasize about the story of their birth. They create a mythical mother and father, a fairy tale with a happy ending. I never did that, never felt the need to. I had a wonderful life, two loving parents, and I lacked for nothing. Yet deep down, as I soon discovered, there was a side of me I'd been ignoring.

The child who cried herself to sleep on nights when Mom and Dad were out, terrified they wouldn't come back...the schoolgirl who wore the badge of adoption like a gold star, almost ashamed, not wanting to be different...the young teen who looked in the mirror and wondered whose eyes stared back at her.

For that girl to ever grow up, I needed to do this. To face down closed doors weathered with age, bolted shut with locks so rusted it would take a miracle to open.

But that's exactly what I got. A miracle. I can say without doubt that every detail of my search and reunion was just that—a God-ordained miracle—even the painful parts. And there was pain. More than I could have anticipated.

Once my birth mother was located (alarmingly easily), I decided to write her a letter. I had all her contact information, including e-mail and phone number, but I had no idea what I was getting into or who I was introducing myself to.

No reply came, and family and friends were understandably cautious. I should have been wary, but I was too consumed, too driven by an inexplicable, innate need to know. I *had* to know. So I threw caution to the wind and fired off an e-mail. Fully justified of course, because if she wasn't the right person, didn't I need to know that?

She was.

The first e-mail I received from my birth mother was not flowery, not gushing with joy at my having found her. It was a simple statement of the facts. My letter was a shock to her, I had nothing medically to be concerned about, and she was not in a position to acknowledge me.

But, but... *You don't even know me!* I wanted to scream. Tell her I was no threat, I was a good person, a woman of faith, successful, married to a wonderful man with two amazing kids that shared her bloodline. But she was clearly not interested. And I was stunned. Because, in all my agonizing over whether searching was the right thing to do, it never occurred to me that *the woman who gave me life might not want to be found.*

I don't give up easily. Not when I really want something. And I really wanted to know her. To know her story. To know mine. They say be careful what you wish for. They're right.

Eventually, we established a somewhat tenuous e-mail relationship. I liken that time now as to being an addict—so desperate for the next response, longing for that cold exterior to crack, praying for her to move past conversations about the weather. For her to give me the answers I pleaded for.

Through all the pain, confusion, and heartache, it was sometimes hard to remember God was in this. Friends carried me along on prayers and hugs and shoulders to cry on. Some days it felt like being rejected all over again. Being held at arm's length, only allowed a glimpse into the life of this stranger who'd chosen to give me life when she could easily have taken another path.

A year and a half into this strange, surreal relationship, she lowered the shield. I discovered I had a half-sister, nieces, and a nephew.

And none of them knew I existed.

My birth mother wanted to keep it that way.

So I had another choice to make. All my life I'd longed for this, a sister to share secrets and joys and sorrows with. But did I have the right to barge in on her life? Did she have the right to know me? My birth mother thought not.

God disagreed.

In the end, I was given what I did not deserve. Now, eleven years after the fact, my sister and I know we were part of a grander plan. A course set out for us from the beginning, paths that would eventually merge like they'd never been parted.

Perhaps the bigger miracle was the day I stood in my birth mother's living room, met her eyes, identical to my own, and watched her come toward me, arms outstretched. It was the first and last hug I received from her, as she died five months after our first meeting.

But all things come full circle, and I believe she got the closure she needed. So did I. And I received so much more...inner peace, puzzle pieces that finally fit together, and new family members to call my own.

God is indeed very, very good.

CATHERINE WEST is an award-winning author who writes stories of hope and healing from her island home in Bermuda. Her first novel, *Yesterday's Tomorrow*, released in 2011 and won the INSPY for Romance, a Silver Medal in the Reader's Favorite Awards, and was a finalist in the Grace Awards. Catherine's second novel, *Hidden in the Heart*, released in September 2012, was long listed in the 2012 INSPY's and was a finalist in the 2013 Grace Awards.

When she's not at the computer working on her next story, you can find her taking her Border Collie for long walks or tending to her roses and orchids. She and her husband have two grown children. Catherine is a member of American Christian Fiction Writers and Romance Writers of America, and is represented by Rachelle Gardner of Books & Such Literary. Catherine loves to connect with her readers and can be reached at Catherine@catherinejwest.com.

3

In the Shadows

Christine, spring 1997

A couple of weeks later, after numerous drafts, I finish the long, book-like letter for Sarah. There's so much to tell. A short history of my life, how I feel about her, why I chose adoption for her, why I want to meet her, how God has comforted me over the years, and the story of the mysterious pink flowers that I always received near her birthday.

Since it's a fair distance to Bob's office, I wrap the journal in a large brown envelope and entrust it to a friend from church who has a counseling session with him this week. She's happy to deliver the letter for me.

Because it was a small, local Christian agency that arranged the private adoption all those years ago, I figure it'll be a snap for Bob to find Sarah. So I wait every day, expecting the phone to ring, to hear Bob say, "Sarah wants to meet you."

But for the first time since I've known Bob, he doesn't return my calls. Has he delivered my letter to Sarah and her family yet? Each night I fight off the fear of rejection, imagining he's delivered the letter but doesn't want to give me the bad news that Sarah doesn't want to meet me.

Several times that spring and summer I leave a number of hesitant voicemail messages to remind Bob that I'm waiting. I keep telling myself, *Don't worry. God has everything under control. Just wait for it.*

In the meantime, I avidly read photocopies of adoption reunion stories that I picked up from a local support group, dog-earing all the happy reunions. Every once in a while I reach for my small journal from 1979 that sits on top of the photocopied stories. The little book falls open to a page where the entries in ballpoint pen have faded, where a fragile pink flower nestles. Any careless touch can cause the flower to crumble. Have I banked all my hopes on something as flimsy as this faded pink petal? Is my hungry mother's heart yearning for something that's not on God's agenda?

Winter passes, and so does Sarah's nineteenth birthday.

One day the following August as I work at the bank, a man strolls up to my wicket. Not one of our clients, this lawyer is dropping off some mortgage papers for a customer. I glance at the name on his business card, then at him. My nerve endings tingle.

I know this man.

Only twice in my life have I seen him. The first time, when I was pregnant with Sarah to start the adoption papers. The second time, after she'd been born and relinquished, I returned to his office to finalize my severing of all legal rights to my baby. Nineteen years ago. I've not seen this lawyer since.

But today he stands at my wicket.

With a stutter I tell him who I am. His stoic expression transforms with a smile as he asks about my life. I rush my telling, and he's so pleased things turned out well for me, and asks if I've ever seen Sarah or her family. This shakes me. *People really do expect reunions to happen.*

"I'm searching for her right now."

"Any success?"

"No. Bob Trainor—you remember Bob—I talked to him a while back. He might be able to find his old files on Sarah's adoption."

And I wait, breathless. There's a reason this lawyer came to my wicket. He could have gone to any of the other staff, but he came to me. So it's no surprise when he plops his glasses on his nose, pulls out his pen, and writes on the back of his business card. "This is the government agency you need to contact—the Vital Statistics Office. Apply to them for the official adoption file. It will give you Sarah's legal name."

Maybe I'm losing that naiveté that spurred me to dash off that first letter to Sarah and then sit back in my living room, a cup of tea pressed between my hands, waiting for the phone to ring. I'm more wary now. Is my conviction that God will bring Sarah back into my life opposed to common sense? I certainly don't want to be reminded of any reunion stories that turn out badly.

At home that night, instead of applying to the Vital Statistics Office, I hesitate. If God isn't bringing this reunion together quickly, perhaps it's better I don't rush it either. It's bad enough that just searching for Sarah has me imagining dozens of creative ways she could reject me. I can't bear to think what Sarah and her parents might go through when they receive my letter. Will they feel threatened by me?

It's better to wait. Let the Lord prepare their hearts for his perfect timing so that no one gets hurt, so that no one feels rejected. Somewhat piously, I prayerfully wait another two months before mailing the application for the adoption file, assuming it will be several more months before I receive an answer. I want to give God all the time he needs to set up the reunion.

A few weeks later on a cold November afternoon, just before the bank closes, a woman plunks her baby boy at my wicket. While I take care of her banking, we chat. She shares how she and her husband just adopted this little boy through Hope Adoption, the same organization Sarah had been adopted through. I tell her my story, and we both marvel. Then the 1980's pop song "Sarah" plays over the sound system—a haunting song that always reminds me of *my* Sarah, and the lady at my wicket says, "Adoptive moms like me love birth moms like you." A warm bubble of love envelopes me as I drive home that night.

I'm hardly through the door, just removing my coat, when ten-year-old Robert charges at me with the mail, one of them a thick envelope. "It's looks special," he says, his blue eyes round with wonder.

I rip open the government envelope, my heart marching double-time. So soon? But it *is* the adoption file. I should have known. God always prepares me for big moments like this with something special—the song "Sarah" at work, the woman and her adopted baby, his love messages...like the mysterious pink flowers that arrive each year around her birthday. God really is answering my prayers. I sweep my little Robert into a big hug, rewarded by his giggle, and rush up the stairs two at a time to read the file in private.

The envelope crackles as I open it on David's and my bed. With shaking hands, I spread the papers out on the bedspread. With reverence, I touch the first tangible evidence of my firstborn. Twenty years I've waited.

The first document is a copy of the live birth registration for Sarah Theresa Lindsay, the names I'd given her. I stare at the signature at the bottom of the form. It's strange to see my handwriting so young.

And there in black and white, her legal name, Sarah Marie

VandenBos.

I tremble. There've been only a few moments in my life when joy spikes like this—the day David asked me to marry him, the day I held each of my newborns, the day I told Lana about Sarah. And now this. Now this.

I read the documents over and over again, testing out loud the sound of Sarah's legal name. I want to shout to the neighbors, the world, that at long last I've found my child.

Downstairs a long while later, I cuddle each of my children and share the file with David and Lana in the kitchen. David holds me close and kisses me on the forehead. Lana's eyes shine as she shares a secret smile with me across the table as we eat supper.

Up until this point I've felt the Lord say, "Wait. It's in my timing." In spite of the hunger to be reunited with my birth child jerking me forward—was it inspiration? In spite of my fear of rejection that keeps jerking me back—was it common sense? With this new information the Lord has quickened the pace. As I trundle forward, it won't be much longer that I remain the invisible one in this adoption triad.

A few days later, with the adoption file containing Sarah's and her parents' legal names, I phone the reunion support group. I don't really know what to expect, but I'd like some advice on the next step toward reunion. The resulting rollercoaster of phone calls in one afternoon comes as a shock. As soon as I tell the other member of the support group, she starts a computer search on the voting registry for Anne and Hans VandenBos. Moments later, feeling again like the Cold War spy, I write Sarah's home address down on a pad of paper. What do I do with this? Walk up to their door and ring the bell, and say, "Hi, I'm Sarah's birth mom. Have you been waiting for me as long as I've been waiting for you?"

For half a minute I want to giggle. In reality, I need Bob to smooth the way, and I write him a long letter bringing him up to date. A week later he calls.

When I sit in his office again, Bob's brow puzzles over what could have happened to the first letter I wrote for Sarah. He can't remember receiving it, but my friend assured me she had delivered it. Bob thinks perhaps he stuck it at the back of an old cabinet when he moved some files.

But nothing ever fazes Bob. With a grin, he asks me to write another letter to Sarah. He's also been wondering why he hadn't heard from me since our first talk, and I wonder what happened to the numerous voicemail messages I left him. Is Bob juggling too many counseling cases and put me on the back burner? Had he simply forgotten me? Or maybe Bob has become a bit cavalier doing monumental work, such as taking a baby from one woman to give that baby to another woman. *As cavalier as God*?

It doesn't matter though. On this section of the emotional rollercoaster God must have slowed the process in answer to my prayers, to prepare Sarah and her parents for the reunion. And now God is speeding up the process. I can accept this. After all, God is God. I stuff my previous disappointment down deep. The heavenly Father isn't going to let me down like my earthly dad did.

Meanwhile, Bob leans back in his chair with a chuckle and fills me in on memories he'd been unable to share with me at the time I relinquished Sarah. Nineteen years earlier, Bob and his wife had taken care of Sarah in their apartment at Trinity Western University. It comes as a surprise to me that Bob and Beverly cared for my child the first night she'd been apart from me. I'd always assumed they'd taken her directly from me to her adoptive parents. A slim shaft of hurt arrows through my ribcage, cutting off my breath. As if I'd been kept in the dark all those years ago. When Bob had phoned me that night after I'd come home from hospital I had no idea my baby slept in his arms.

If I'd known then, would I have asked for her back?

But I shake off this tiny sense of betrayal. It no longer matters. Now the search is back on track, and I can afford to laugh.

Bob smiles over the memory of his own two little girls wheeling the newborn Sarah in a baby buggy up and down the hallway of their apartment building the day they waited for Sarah's chosen parents. I envision the scene unfolding like the sun coming out from behind a cloud. That sweet little memory of Bob's erases a tiny bit of that new shadow in me, that sense of loss, knowing now where she'd actually been after I'd said goodbye. I stuff my jealousy deep into a crevice of my heart.

Before I leave Bob's office, he says, "It's only a few weeks until Christmas. Better wait until after New Year to deliver your letter to Sarah and her parents, so we don't intrude upon their family time."

Family time. I nod and smile, but inside I shrivel. I understand. Still, hurt stabs once more that I'm not considered family. And David and our kids aren't family to Sarah either. The desire to run and hide shrouds me again. So much for my confidence of only moments ago. Oh, who am I kidding? The fear of rejection continues to hammer me on the drive home.

During the Christmas holidays I leave a voicemail for Bob that it would be best to call the whole thing off. Better to stay in the shadows, let Sarah live her life without the awkward addition of a birth mother who doesn't really fit into any family dynamic.

Bob calls back that night. "You've trusted God all these years, Christine. Don't stop trusting now."

Remembering back to September, 1978

I wrote in my journal then, "My baby is moving all the time. I want to laugh and tell everyone that my baby is alive and healthy." But too many evenings I cried.

Late one night as I struggled to sleep, I left my bed to sit in my darkened living room. How was all this stress going to affect my baby? I'd read that expectant mothers talked or sang to their unborn children. I sure didn't feel like singing. All I ever did on the nights I couldn't sleep was cry and pray on my knees in the dark, my arms around my tummy, protecting my baby. Would my child's personality be influenced by my emotions? Or would something of my growing faith in God be passed through to my baby during these long sessions on my knees, in some spiritual sense?

I could get through the next five months of pregnancy. My boss kept my job at the buying office safe for me. But what about after? I had to decide the best thing to do for my baby and me.

In my Bible I'd read about a woman named Hannah. Thinking that no one saw her, she cried her prayer to the Lord. "If you will only look on your servant's misery and remember me...I will give him to the LORD for all the days of his life..."

My heart constricted. "Oh God, adoption? No!" Tears came again, hot and blinding. It was bad enough going through the pregnancy alone, but to give up my child afterward? "I can't do it, Lord. I can't give up my baby."

My vision shimmered as I looked into the dark living room. During the day I felt God's care for me through the people around me, people at the office, my mother.

But now I sensed him here with me. Something almost physical.

I shook my head. It must be my emotional stress. To my thinking, many of the visions people received were constructed from their vivid imaginations. Still, in the corner of my apartment I thought I could almost see him, standing between me and the window, with the night beyond.

Jesus?

"Trust me."

A few weeks later when autumn rains hissed on the road, cars raced up the busy street. I shivered and pulled the collar of my coat tighter, opened my umbrella, and walked toward the office of Burden Bearers.

I skirted a puddle on the sidewalk, almost bumping into a stranger. Was there an alternative to adoption? My mother, one of the bravest people I'd ever known, raised us three kids herself. But no matter how hard she tried, her one salary wasn't enough. We'd never taken vacations, and Mum had always gone without so we kids could have the clothes we needed. But that wasn't the worst.

A child needed a father, didn't they?

Otherwise they turned out like me, lacking confidence, lacking security, and making stupid mistakes like having unprotected sex outside of marriage. People seemed to grow up happier if they had a dad in their life. My mind dictated a clarification—people grew up happier if they had a dad in their life who didn't let them down. A father who didn't forget them.

Rain pinged on the taut umbrella as I searched for the address. I stopped at a red light. If only a husband waited for me on the horizon, a young man waiting to walk over the next hill. But if there was, he wasn't coming on time. He might never come.

The light switched to green, and I joined the crowd crossing the street. I ached to give birth to my baby, kiss bruised toddler knees, meet the teacher on the first day of school, and celebrate graduation. I wanted to be my child's mom. I could muddle through somehow, but muddling along wasn't good enough. As my baby's mother, it was my responsibility to do the very best for my child.

But if I chose adoption, I'd be little more to my baby than these strangers passing me on the street. And as my child grew, would he or she ever feel rejected by me?

Back and forth, my thoughts thrust me one way and then another.

The glass and metal building stood before me. On the second floor, I entered the reception office where calm Christian music played softly. I soaked in the atmosphere, thirsty for this tantalizing promise of peace. Warmth infused me as I listened to the receptionist's farewells to people as they left the office. They walked out the door with hope stamped on their faces. My little one moved inside me as I sat in the waiting room. I rubbed my tummy to caress my child and looked out at the rain slanting on the gray street below. If I went through with this, my baby and I would only have these few months together. Only a few short months to treasure.

"Christine?"

A tall, athletic man in his thirties entered the waiting room. Bob Trainor's smile said everything was going to be all right. I wished I had his kind of confidence. Inside his office, he leaned back in his chair and smiled again. "So, how can I help you?"

"I want you to find parents for my baby," I blurted. "It doesn't matter to me the color of their eyes, where they come from, or what they do for a living. I've come to realize that I want a Christian life for both my child and myself. So, it only matters that the...that the adoptive parents believe in Jesus Christ. They—both of them—must act like Jesus wants people to act. To be real Christians, to, to..." That feeling of being a mother tiger, ready to do anything for the sake of my cub, shrank to that of a weak kitten. "If you can't assure me of that, then I'd be better off keeping my baby."

Bob leaned forward, bracing his elbows on his knees. "Through a new organization we've just started, Hope Adoption, we can arrange an adoption like you've described. I can have several portfolios for you in a month."

The sensation of an elevator dropping shuddered inside me. It was real now. There were couples who wanted my baby. Did *I* want this? I held tears back, drawing on everything within me to keep up my in-control front.

"And what about you?" Bob asked softly.

"Me?"

"You're hurting."

My throat closed. I was so sick of crying, but I couldn't keep up the frail barrier much longer.

"Your heavenly Father loves you, Christine. He watches over you all the time. He never leaves you, and he has great plans for you, if you'll trust him."

Hot tears squeezed out of my eyes.

Bob offered me a box of tissues. "Tell me about you, about the father of your baby. Tell me more about the parents you want for your child."

At the end of my appointment I smiled my thanks to the receptionist, feeling that same hope eddy through me that I'd seen in the other clients. I shrugged into my coat and took my umbrella from the stand. Slowly walking down the street that I'd rushed up earlier, I noticed the rain had eased to a gentle mist. I folded my umbrella down and raised my face, letting the spray rest on my eyelids and cheeks. Soft droplets—kisses from my so-called heavenly Father?

Did I fancy these as a promise from where he sat so high above?

No young husband waited on the horizon for me. Instead, after today there would be two strangers standing on the rim of my life. I didn't know them, but God did. Two people my little one would call Mom and Dad. A tiny foot or elbow moved inside me. If only there was another way.

But even now, I sensed God choosing this couple in the shadows that would remain unknown to me. God listened to their prayers as intently as he listened to mine. Because they would be my baby's parents, I loved them. This man and this woman were my brother and my sister, a special family God was putting together through adoption.

From Manitoba Canada—The Adoption of Levi
"A Most Unexpected Reunion"
by adoptive mother Cheryl Unrau

Our adoption journey ended in the sweetest and most unexpected of reunions. Like all adoptions, our journey began with loss—but not the usual loss of giving up a child or being infertile. My husband Derek and I, and our two children born to us, were the so-called "guinea pigs" to an overseas adoption program based an already successful one initiated in neighboring provinces. We were so sure God was leading us to this program that we gave consent to our agency, and they proceeded with our dossier.

We were infused with enthusiasm as answers to specific prayers came to fruition. From the pocketbook to the paper work, progression was nearly effortless. Our provision was positively providential. There was no doubt in our minds that we were in the Lord's will.

So convinced were we that God was going to give us an adopted child, we even selected a name. Though we were open to receiving a boy or a girl, we felt strongly about the name Levi. It was a beautifully kept secret between God and Derek and me. I prayed the name Levi with diligence, covering all facets of adoption and transition I could think of.

With two biological children, Alexa and Mason, I prayed for their acceptance of another sibling, those prayers circling them in hugs. We were so excited waiting for the completion of our family. The kids discussed how they would rearrange their rooms to house their new brother or sister.

I anticipated the arrival of our third child like any expectant mother. Though the wait was more that of an elephant's gestation than the typical nine-month pregnancy, it did not deter my excitement. I seized the opportunity to share reports of adoption progress with everyone I knew, drawing others into my orb of enthusiasm.

But, in one phone call, after three years of working and waiting, with only a few spoken words over the line, I felt my heart drop to the pit of my stomach and a lethargic melancholy followed. After years of chasing, praying, hoping, and speaking words of faith out loud, our pursuit of overseas adoption met its end. Man's best efforts could not overcome the red tape. Our adoption was closed. Our little Levi would never arrive.

My initial response was disbelief. Surely, this was just a misunderstanding. But as realization dawned, my tears flowed to signal the start of a myriad of emotions. I retreated into a pit of shame and anger—shame at my public boasting and anger toward God.

After many weeks of throwing a trashy tirade before the Lord, I began to see the filth in the dry well of my soul.

How did this happen? When had I replaced my relationship with God with religion and a holier-than-thou-attitude, so that in the face of this huge disappointment in my life I berated him? I was so sure he wanted me to be an adoptive mother. Derek, Alexa, Mason, and I would have done everything to provide the warmest, most loving home for Levi. But God had failed to fulfill what I thought was his promise of a child.

I succumbed to the bitter, resentful anger that accompanies being hurt. I questioned where I had gone wrong, how I had misunderstood, what I had left incomplete, and if God had something personal against me. I wondered if he thought I would make a poor adoptive parent. Or if I was already shabby at mothering and this was a form of discipline.

With the brokenness of loss, I turned my feet to the wilderness of sorrow like that of the Israelites as they plodded in the dust, following an obscure pillar of cloud.

Ravenously, I consumed the Scriptures and relied on the Lord for my living water of joy and peace. The pain of surrender to my loss and God's ultimate will was acute—I buried myself in my Bible and hung on to any form of teaching that would lead me through the desert. I found company in the complaining and grumbling of God's chosen people, and I even turned to the book of Job to find comfort in the fact that I was not the only one who felt duped. I spent many hours reminding myself of God's sovereignty. I was so confused. The sudden change of plans did not look like the future I had envisioned.

God had not decreed that we would adopt a child. Unlike birth mothers, I'd not had to give up a baby. Unlike many adoptive parents who couldn't have children biologically, I had two sweet kids who filled my heart and life with joy. But the searing loss that I would not be the mother of an adopted child consumed me.

And I so wanted to be Levi's mother. I would picture our family hug on African soil. I envisioned dark faces, our family so eager to spot the one that was going to add a branch to our family tree. I would inwardly smile as I tried to imagine the coarse texture of tight curly hair and cherish the thought of toddler giggles. I knew the transition would be tough, but we were willing to give it our very best. My heart ached to give a family and a home to a needy child.

Instead, our adoption journey ended in the sweetest and most unexpected of reunions.

God reaffirmed my acceptance into his family through that grand adoption paid by the cross of Christ. He is doing a new thing in me—"making a way in the desert of my loss and a stream in the wasteland" (Isaiah 43:19). My passion for a thriving family is not daunted but fueled and renewed even more so by my adoptive Father. My family is complete in him.

And God is more than able. Through my contribution to this book, I am reminded that he can raise the dead and bring old dreams back to life. Continually, I remind myself to delight in him. It took the Israelites forty years to reach their promised land. I dare not limit what my Lord can do. All—loss and gain—is good in his hands and in his timing. Because of his goodness, and in his timing, God used our passion for family and the African culture to recently draw us into serving him on the mission field, fulfilling all of his promises and allowing us to spread his love abroad and across all nations.

4

Pendulum of Faith

Christine, January, 1999

At the bank, customers line up from the door to the wickets, but I look up from the paycheck on my blotter to the woman making this deposit. She raises an eyebrow. "Gail?" I ask. "You're Gail, aren't you?"

"Yes, Christine, you do know me." She quirks a half-smile. "How long's it been?"

"Twenty years." With Sarah's birthday looming, I don't need Gail to do the math. Gail and Rod used to double date with Jim and me. We'd seen the movie *The Goodbye Girl* together in 1978, but since I relinquished Sarah, I've not seen Jim or any of his friends.

It takes Gail and me a few moments to get over our amazement. How all this time they've been doing their banking at my branch and yet we've never met; how we've both been married and raising children in Maple Ridge and never bumped into each other. Eventually I get around to asking the question that clangs in my mind. "Do you keep in touch with Jim? How's he doing?" For years I've imagined him married, hopefully to some nice woman, with kids of his own.

Her eyes get big with sympathy. "That's why I didn't tell you who I was right away. I didn't know how to bring it up. Jim's dead, Christine. He died last August, quietly in his sleep from a heart attack."

That hollow feeling of going warm and cold at the same time streams through my veins. Something inside me goes forever silent. As I listen, Gail fills me in. Jim never married. He had no children other than Sarah.

Jim's dead. After Gail leaves I ask my supervisor for a break. Up in the lunchroom, I cry. All these years later I weep for the young man I used to love. If Sarah had never been conceived, I doubt I'd have given him the place in my heart that he owned. David has been all the husband I ever wanted or needed, but Jim and I were linked by Sarah's life. The loss of him in this world burrows a dark empty pocket inside my chest, a phantom sort of loss, much as our daughter is a phantom to me.

I walk home from work, hardly aware of my surroundings. During the last year of the search, I assumed that if Sarah wanted to meet me, she would also want to meet her father. I've always hoped to help her find him. Now Jim and Sarah will never meet. If our reunion day ever does come, will I have the solemn task of telling her of her birth father's passing? As I walk the remaining blocks home, I pray for her and try to imagine how Sarah will feel when she learns that her birth father has died, as I've imagined what she's doing and thinking at various times of her life—playing as a little child, swimming in the summertime, starting high school.

And what on earth does she think of me or her birth father? Does she ever think of Jim or me? And the big question—if Bob has contacted Sarah's family, what does she think of the pretty journal with the blue and pink hydrangeas? Or the photos of her brothers

Kyle and Robert and her sister Lana? Or the slender gold chain with the pink pearl for her birthday that Lana helped me wrap?

It's been two months since Bob and I talked before Christmas. If God is slowing the pace again, it's because he's answering my prayers, preparing everyone's heart for our reunion. I share these upbeat thoughts with my friends, but not some of my darker thoughts—thoughts that I don't even share with David, but write in my journal. "I'm sorry, Lord, but I don't care what the law says. One set of adoptive parents does not nullify the biological parents. It's not natural for me to continually suppress my maternal feelings and be this invisible thing called a birth mother."

Adding to my mixed emotions over Jim's passing, that is hard for me to admit—even with all the counseling Bob gave me after the relinquishment in 1979, even with all that I've read and gathered from the adoption reunion support group. But the truth stares me down. For the past twenty years I've secretly considered myself sharing Sarah with her adoptive parents. That when God put their family together, somehow I was still part of that family—albeit a small part, invisible and out on the fringes.

Whoa, I can just about hear everyone in the adoption triad around the world gasp.

I imagine the frowns, the soft scolding of adoption experts. "You as a birth mother have not completely grieved your relinquishment. You have not fully accepted your position as birth mother." And so on and so on.

How on earth am I supposed to feel and act like a birth mother? What the blazes is a birth mother anyway? Is she like an aunt? A mother-in-law? A friend?

Idiot, I call myself, dreaming that my family and I can slip into a special role as relatives in Sarah's extended family, and them in ours. Idiot! Because again, there's no word from Bob.

But then a memory of Sarah's middle name pops into my head—Theresa—not her legal middle name, but the one I gave her. Over Christmas, while I'd been studying the Book of Ruth, I learned that the name Theresa means "harvester." Harvesting is all about timing, seasons, and patience while nature does its work.

As I look back on 1998, there are too many coincidences. My first letter to Sarah, hidden in Bob's office and from his memory, and how God gave me peace over that delay. Then the lawyer dropping into my branch that August day to inform me of how to apply for the adoption file, the very same month Jim died in his sleep.

God slows the pace. God quickens the pace. Why can't my emotions rest in his timing? Why must I always swing like a pendulum, faith tugging one way, emotions another? Have I cast common sense to the wind and taken up the fanaticism I fear, when a person can't accept their loss? Or is it possible that some things happen simply in response to circumstances? Bob's a busy man and might have forgotten me. So what? My first journal-type letter to Sarah was lost. Okay. While God works out his plans and promises, he might not necessarily interfere with everything we humans do as if we were puppets on his strings.

Dear Lord in heaven, I hate my desperation. The constant longing and disappointment drains me, only to have guilt nag me as well. I'm afraid that lately I've not been a very good mom to my other three kids. I'm there with them every day, cooking their meals, providing for them, giving them extra hugs, but am I as consumed with their emotional needs as I am with my own?

But I can't think about that now. The kids seem fine. They must be fine. It's me who's standing on a thin ledge, as I block the word "obsession" from my mind.

Throughout December the story of Ruth drew me in. If Sarah and I ever do meet, in no way do I want to detract from Sarah's relationship with her parents. As if I could anyway. But tenderness grew between Ruth and Naomi even though Naomi hadn't raised Ruth. The more I think of it, the relationship between a daughter-in-law and mother-in-law resembles best what I hope for Sarah and me. Not Mother...but a type of mother?

My imagination soars with the biblical account. On a hot, dry, dusty day in Moab where famine rages, Ruth prepares to leave her people and the place she's buried her husband to trudge all the way to Bethlehem with her mother-in-law. I imagine her clinging to Naomi and howling out her sobs. "Take me with you. I want your people to be my people. I want your God to be my God. I want us to be family forever."

So off they go. Naomi means "pleasantness." Ruth—"friend." Two women, a mother figure and a daughter, arriving in Bethlehem just as the barley harvest begins. Perfect timing, since the harvest is their only way to survive.

My head tells me God is doing the same thing in my life. But the pendulum of my faith and emotions keep swinging.

I trusted you, Lord, when I gave her up. Why can't I trust you today?

Remembering back to January, 1979

I looked forward to my sessions with Bob. Each time I left his office, my faith lifted. Today I waited in reception, again listening to the same warm inspirational music played low. I caressed my tummy. There was no movement. Baby slept dreamlessly.

My devotions this morning were from Galatians 3:6: "Don't these things happen among you just as they happened with Abraham? He believed God, and that act of belief was turned into a life that was right with God" (MSG). I was doing the same today, taking an unfathomable leap of faith by making plans to give up my child. Like Abraham...and Isaac.

My thoughts dissolved like a chalk drawing on a rain-swept sidewalk as Bob stepped out to reception and ushered me into his office. He still wore that maddening smile that said everything was going to be all right. At eight months pregnant I lumbered to the chair by the window, borrowing Bob's faith that there would be joy at the end of this heartache for both my baby and me. He filled his favorite chair that leaned way back. "I've got three portfolios for you."

My pulse sped up. He began to outline three different couples. All of them sounded great, exactly the kind of parents I wanted for my child. All lived in the Fraser Valley, but of course Bob couldn't tell me what cities they lived in. All were committed Christians, serious about their faith. How on earth was I to choose? Sure I'd prayed for direction, but how could I know?

A long while later, as if he'd been merely warming up, Bob continued, "And this particular lady recently left her teaching position because she believes God will give her a baby this year."

I lifted my chin as my baby dozed beneath my ribcage. This woman had faith. I considered myself a woman of faith. Young, oh yes, gullible, unwise a great deal of the time, but willing to give up my baby because it was best for my child. Didn't that count as the step-out-on-mid-air-trust that God rewarded? The kind of faith that believed he was good, like old Abraham believed when he left his home, packed up all his belongings and family, without a clue where God was leading him. It also seemed to be the same sort of faith I shared with this woman, and I wanted a woman with that kind of faith raising my child.

With more bravado than I felt, I said, "She's the one."

"What?"

"The lady who gave up her teaching job on faith. I choose her. That couple."

Bob sputtered. "Aren't you making your decision too quickly? What about this other couple—"

"No. What you said about her sparked something inside me. That's the mom and dad I want for my baby."

I walked out of Bob's office that day with sure steps and a wobbly smile. I'd made my decision based on faith, just like Abraham. The heavenly Father was going to make it turn out all right. God wasn't in the business of breaking hearts.

From the Fraser Valley, Canada—The Adoption of Sarah
"God Blesses the Motherless with Children"
By adoptive mother Anne VandenBos

My monthly cycle stopped at age fourteen. I just lived without it, certainly never missing it. Until I was madly in love with Hans. We had dated for five years. He proposed to me one warm September day, and we planned to shop together for a ring and get married in December. I was in the second year of my teaching career and we could go on our honeymoon to Disneyland in California during my two week Christmas break. I told Hans it might not be possible for me to have children. He wanted to marry me in spite of that possibility.

For three months, nobody knew that Hans and I were planning our wedding. The money Hans had saved for an engagement ring had to be used to pay for one of his speeding tickets. I found white French silk velvet to make my wedding dress—perfect for a December wedding—and bought the same fabric in sky blue for my four bridesmaids, and purple for the flower girl. I also bought maroon brocade to sew my going away suit. I hid all of it in the trunk of my car.

In late November we got our wedding rings and shocked our parents with the news of our marriage in just four weeks. They gave us their blessing and a beautiful wedding. What a rush, with a bridal shower almost every weekend. And we needed to find furniture and an apartment to rent. I focused on sewing every spare moment, and I taught full time.

I think most people thought I was pregnant because of the short notice for our wedding. Little did they know how cautious and modest Hans was in this regard.

But all of our siblings had children. People didn't realize how their comments hurt. Like my mom who believed it's so much easier to get pregnant at a young age. Much as I love her, if I heard her say that one more time, I'd scream! With any extremely frustrating relative, you can't help wondering, "How can someone I love so much, upset me?" Mom had given birth to her first child at the age of sixteen, so that's what she based her belief on.

Hans and I yearned for a family for a long time. But after many medical tests, I received confirmation that I could not conceive. God's reason was that he had adoption plans for us.

"He gives children to the childless wife, so that she becomes a happy mother" (Psalm 113:9 TLB).

One day I sat alone at my dining room table, crying out to the Lord because of my heartache for a family. The presence of the Holy Spirit poured over me. A warm heat spread across my shoulders, comforting me. My tears dried completely as God's promise washed over me that we would get the family we longed for. From that day on, a song played in my heart. I knew God would provide.

In August of 1971, I saved my church bulletin that told about a Christian American Adoption Agency. I started praying that a Christian adoption agency would begin in Canada. The Lord dried my tears many times over the next seven years.

In August 1978, we received a monthly newsletter from Burden Bearers saying that adoptive homes were needed for some older children. We wrote them a letter saying we would like to apply for adoption. When we went for our interview with Bob Trainor that September, he shared the stories of two families of three children each whose mothers had died. We never asked for a baby because we thought it might take too long to wait for one. We told Bob we would open our home to as many as three children under the age of seven, boys or girls. We wanted to take whoever God wanted for us.

We thought we might get one of those families before Christmas, so we bought our five-bedroom home because our other house had only three bedrooms and a pool in the backyard—a safety concern with small children. But in the end, the one family went to the grandparents, and the father of the other family came up from California to take his three children. However, that promise from God, that he would provide the family we longed for, didn't diminish. That song in my heart only grew louder, reaching a crescendo.

My family would begin soon.

Here is a portion from 1 Samuel 1: "In her deep anguish Hannah prayed to the Lord, weeping bitterly. And she made a vow, saying,

'Lord Almighty, if you will only look on your servant's misery and remember me, and not forget your servant but give her a son, then I will give him to the Lord for all the days of his life...'

"And Eli answered, 'Go in peace, and may the God of Israel grant you what you have asked of him.'"

5

Another Birthday Comes and Goes

Christine, February 1999

I pass a plate of cookies around my sister-in-law's miniscule living room during her candle party. It's hard not to listen to the conversations of her work friends, and my ears perk up when I hear, "Have you ever thought of searching for your birth mother?"

My full attention latches on to two young women talking on the sofa. The other answers, "No, she's not really anything to me. I've never had any desire to meet her."

"My husband doesn't want to meet his birth mother either," the other girl says. "It's just not something he wants to do. You never know what you'll find if you go down that road."

The adoptee laughs. "My birth mother named me Phyllis. She obviously didn't want me, saddling me with a name like that. Thank God my parents changed it."

Sitting on the edge of my chair, I cringe for the absent birth mother. I imagine her pain. Maybe that other birth mom named her baby after her mother or a beloved grandmother. To me, the fact that the other birth mother named her baby told a heart load of stories, and my back stiffens with outrage on her behalf. I probably should mind my own business, but as usual I plunge in where angels shudder and lean over with what I hope is a warm smile. "Maybe these two birth mothers are nice, ordinary people. I'm a birth mom, and right now I'm searching for my birth daughter."

I was right. I should have minded my own business. Their frosty looks numb me, and they return to their private conversation without a word in my direction. I take what refuge I can, pull back against the wall, wishing I could fade into the paintwork. Serves me right. Lately I feel as if I'm on a soapbox. Given any opportunity, I'll spew forth on my perceived plight of poor invisible birth mothers who need to come out of the shadows. All I need is a placard. And I'm not sure I like myself in this role, especially when I'm well aware that my own plans are skewed by a capped-off geyser of emotion.

And Sarah's twentieth birthday, February 24th, comes and goes.

Bitterness creeps in as I write in my journal, "Dear Lord, the anticipation of meeting Sarah by this birthday was intense. Church on Sunday was very hard. The worship music and my love for you always pulls my barriers down. I did banking calculations in my head to keep from crying. But when Krystal (an adopted girl) got up to play the piano and sing, it was too much. I left the auditorium to cry in the bathroom."

As I walk to work two days after Sarah's birthday I mutter under my breath, "It's all my imagination, isn't it? All those years of you doing something special around her birthday to share it with me." I stumble over my feet as I quicken my pace. "Just my overactive imagination, isn't it, Lord? All those years of mysterious pink flowers—stupid flowers indeed! And songs on the radio at exactly the right time, people popping out of the woodwork—all me seeing what I want to see."

But the blasted tears squeeze out no matter how hard I try to shove them back. "Have you led me to search for Sarah? Or am I a fool who should settle for reality and stop dreaming dreams? You have forgotten about me, haven't you?"

At work that day I am a bear. For the past year my co-workers at the bank have shared in every successful milestone as I searched for Sarah, every crushing disappointment. They know the significance of the date that's just passed.

As I struggle to paste a smile on my face for the next customer, I notice my supervisor, Linda, leave the bank. Before closing, from the corner of my eye, I see Linda slip up beside me. She sets a potted plant, a pink Kalanchoe wrapped in shiny pink foil, on the counter beside me. Dark green waxy leaves stage the perfect background for a myriad of tiny, star-shaped pink blooms. Though the girls at the bank know about the search, they do not know the significance of the color of these flowers. Linda could have picked white daisies, yellow roses, blue violets, anything.

All anger seeps from me as each tiny pink bloom shouts in silent indignation, "See...he has never forgotten you!"

Like I've done for the past twenty years, I wish Sarah a happy birthday, a message that I pray God will convey to her over the forty miles that separate us, the way he talks to me through these blossoms. That Sarah will look up in the midst of her day and know beyond all understanding that her birth mother is thinking of her. Sending her love.

Remembering back to February 24, 1979

I'd written in my journal the morning after Sarah's birth, "I was amazed when I heard her cry, but not surprised. I'd been saying *her* for months. When I saw her face I fell in love. I couldn't take my eyes off her. Right away, she was Sarah. The nurse wrapped her in a yellow blanket and gave her to me. Her eyes were open, and for the first time I really knew who she was. How pretty she was. I nearly drowned in her eyes."

In many ways, at twenty-one, I was as unaware as my baby. Under the impression that my adoption plan for Sarah meant I had no right to see her after the delivery, I'd never even thought to ask. That first morning I lay in my hospital bed with the drape closed around me, in vain blocking out the sounds of other mothers in the ward caring for their babies. Squeezing my eyes shut, curled in a fetal position, I listened to my baby's cry all the way down the hall in the nursery. Surely that had to be Sarah. Less than twenty-four hours old, and yet I recognized her cry.

A nurse pushed aside the curtain to check on me. "Don't you want to get your baby?" she gently queried.

Very quietly I explained, "But I'm giving her up for adoption."

"I know." She laid a soft hand on my shoulder.

I weakened with her kindness. "I'm not sure what happens...I suppose my counselor will come soon and tell me. I've called him."

"But you can take care of her until then."

"I can? Can I?" Time stood still.

She smiled and, nodding, lifted her brows. "She's your baby."

I suppose I experienced the pain of contracting muscles, but I don't recall any. I do remember trotting down that hallway as fast as my feet could carry me. Stopping outside the nursery to catch my breath, I listened. A baby did cry. The only baby left in the nursery as all the others were with their mothers. That was my baby in there.

I pushed the door open and raced to her bassinette. Lifting her into my arms, up close to my face, I breathed in the heavenly sweetness. Enfolded the softness of her like a baby bird's wing next to my heart. She stopped crying, and I carried her to the rocker to sit and hold her. To cherish, to cradle her warm and close.

A little pink rosebud, fragile, with golden down on her head. I had never seen anything so beautiful.

I had no idea when Bob would come. No idea of the next step. But for as long as I had, I would be her mother. For not one minute would Sarah be without a mother's love.

From The Fraser Valley, Canada—The Adoption of Sarah
"Our Daughter's Name"
By adoptive mother Anne VandenBos

In the midst of a teaching day in February 1979, I got the call that Bob had a baby girl for us. Joy overwhelmed me.

The next time Bob called, he asked me if we had thought about a name for the baby. I said we were thinking of either Elizabeth or Sarah.

Bob said, "The birth mom has been calling her Sarah."

"Well that settles it. We'll name her Sarah."

6

I Saw Her Face

Christine, March 13, 1999

The '80s pop song "Sarah" wavers on the sound system again while I'm at work. I last heard that song back in November, the day the adoption file arrived in the mail. Today, the haunted tinny repetition of the name *Sarah...Sarah...* annoys me, and I wish somebody would just turn it off.

When my shift ends, David is waiting in the parking lot. "I've got good news." He drives out, heading toward the mall. "Lana's on the Honor Roll."

"Whooopeee!" Something to celebrate.

We race around the stores and rush to pick up a gift, cake, Chinese food, and balloons, and then we hurry home again to the kids. As a family, in the kitchen we're making a considerable dent in the chop suey and chow mien when the phone rings. In the midst of loud chatter, I hear only half of what David says as he answers the phone. I nurse a hot cup of tea in my hands and sit back like a satisfied cat in a warm patch of sunlight, enjoying my kids, relishing this moment for Lana. I couldn't be prouder of my daughter.

David covers the receiver and mouths, "It's for you."

Bob's calming voice comes over the phone. He's given Sarah's parents the photocopy that I provided of the journal I'd written to Sarah. He's also met with Sarah's dad. That very day! My heart skips a beat. My actual letter in the pretty journal and the gift Lana helped me choose are at long last on their way to Sarah. Hardly able to breathe, I let Bob's voice fill my ear. "Sarah's mom gave me a letter for you, and it's got pictures of Sarah."

"I'll be at your office tomorrow to get it."

Bob chuckles. "You want to wait that long? I'll meet you halfway at the McDonald's in Pitt Meadows."

"Okay." It's hard to catch my breath.

Bob's tone turns dry. "Of course, if you want to wait until tomorrow...but I'm looking at her picture right now. She's very pretty—"

"No! I want them tonight." Laughter bursts from me.

"Well, if you're really sure."

My grin must be lighting up the kitchen. From across the table Lana sends me a knowing smile. The boys glance up, perplexed, but happily dig into their ice cream and cake. David sits at the end of the table with a similar satisfied-cat smile on his face to the one I had a few moments ago. As soon as I tell him that Bob is meeting us in half an hour, David's satisfied smile dissolves into quick determination as he grabs our coats and ensures the boys do their homework while we're out.

As I whirl about, getting myself ready, Lana comes quietly to me. "Can I come too?"

I hug her close. "Oh yes, yes!" Nothing could make me happier than to share this moment with Lana.

As David, Lana, and I practically fling ourselves out the door—with my heart beating like a drum solo—I lift my face to the night sky and thank God. How extraordinarily sweet of him to arrange this first communication with Sarah's family on the same night that Lana was being honored.

A half hour later at McDonald's we sit down with Bob at one of the hard plastic tables. I feel all three sets of eyes on me as I open the letter from Sarah's mom. I scan the letter, wanting to take it home and read it slower then, to savor it later, but her generosity reaches out, her warm words hug me close. I was right all along. God did entwine our two hearts over Sarah. Anne truly is my sister.

But I can't hold myself back any longer. My fingers close around the small package of pictures. I yearn for a glimpse of Sarah's face again. I'd already confessed to David and Lana that I'd sneaked into Sarah's former high school and saw her grad photo, but I don't have the courage to tell Bob. Though a copy of her graduation portrait is included, it's as though I'm seeing it for the first time. Something invisible shoves me hard in the chest, knocking me off the footings of my life. Did Anne feel a similar shifting in the sphere of her life when she got my letter?

One daughter—two mothers?

With trembling fingers I sift through each picture. Sarah at one month cuddled in some relative's arms, three months smiling toothless on a quilt, one year old sitting in her highchair. On and on...all her life...at four years old playing with her adopted twin brothers, Matthew and Luke. At six in kindergarten, her blond hair done up in pigtails and bows and a gap-toothed grin. At twelve... At fourteen making a silly face for the camera, her long blond hair framing her shoulders. And then a young woman graduating from high school and entering university. In each photo I see a tiny bit of me, but if I'd met her on the street, I wouldn't have recognized her as my child.

It doesn't matter. This is Sarah now. My feet find sure ground again. A whole chunk of my broken heart is mended. Sarah's mom loves me as I love her.

I'm as giddy as I imagine Naomi was when she finally arrived in Bethlehem with Ruth. After their long journey, the whole town turns out, and the women exclaim, "Can this be Naomi?" They remembered her from long ago. They remembered her name. She'd come home. After my long journey toward a reunion with Sarah and her family I play with the idea, *Can this be Christine?* Is this my time at last to become a part of Sarah's family? Have I finally come home?

Bob interrupts my thoughts with a question that pleases me. He asks Lana about her life, and David proudly announces she's on the Honor Roll her graduating year. I beam at Lana over the table, but then I pick up Anne's letter again. My heart stops on a piece of news I'd glossed over in my first reading. Sarah is not only in her second year of university preparing to become a nurse, she's also engaged to be married. Her wedding date is only two months away.

Two months. My soaring joy fizzles out some. It's always been my dream to attend Sarah's wedding. But two months? Does that give us enough time to meet, develop a friendship so that she'll feel comfortable enough to invite me—us—to her wedding?

For the following two weeks I read and re-read Anne's letter. Waiting for that call that Sarah wants to meet me. Chafing each day when there's no word.

On March 23rd, Bob calls. My knees go weak when he says, "Sarah wants to meet you. Can you come on Saturday?"

Two days. Two days, and I'll finally see her face-to-face. Now that my dream hovers on the horizon, my voice loses its strength, tired from the pounding of my heart, the draining of the long search. "Yes, we'll be there Saturday."

Now it was time to tell the boys.

It seems the most momentous announcements I make to my children are on the hard plastic seats of fast food restaurants. This time David, Lana, and I take Kyle and Robert to Dairy Queen. Just like David did with Lana, he clears his throat and says to the boys, "I've got something pretty important to tell you guys."

My sandy haired, fifteen-year-old Kyle, and my blond, ten-year-old Robert look up from their ice cream sundaes.

David shares with them almost verbatim what he told Lana a year ago.

"Huh?" Kyle immediately digs his spoon deeper into his sundae.

Robert's brow crinkles as he stares at me. A long moment later he puts both hands on top of his head, then lowers his forehead to the table, sits up again, and smacks his forehead with an open palm. "You mean I've got another sister?"

Lana gentles her long-suffering huff with a smile and draws out the word, "Yes."

Robert looks more closely at the photos of Sarah, picking one up of her in kindergarten, with her blond hair done up in pigtails and ribbons. "Wow, chop off her curls and she looks just like me."

Kyle remains quiet through all of this, focusing only on his ice cream. Now he interjects, "Hey Dad, can we look at those golf clubs that are on sale at Canadian Tire this week?"

David and I share a long look. I reach out to tousle Kyle's hair, and he rewards me with a contented smile. Kyle's tender heart needs time to adjust to this thunderbolt.

Before leaving Dairy Queen, we tell the boys about Sarah's adopted brothers. Both Kyle and Robert want to know if Matthew and Luke would be interested in playing street hockey with them sometime.

They're so ready to accept this shift in their family orbit. But as much as I love Sarah, if for one minute I thought meeting her would hurt any of my kids, I'd stop everything. The paradox hits me between the eyes. These are my kids. But Sarah is my firstborn, and the distance between us is creating a constantly widening rift in my soul. Still, as much as I crave a relationship with Sarah, I can't even meet her if it risks hurting the children who live safely beneath my roof.

Relief shores me up—my kids *are* reacting positively to the reunion, and the appointment is set. I don't have to make that awful decision, which is good because I'm not sure how much more shifting of my orbit I can take, or how much longer I can deny my maternal feelings for this daughter I relinquished. I've often wondered how God managed to properly love the ninety-nine sheep he left behind to go out searching the hills for that little one that was lost.

Sure, I'd given Sarah up at my own expense for her own good, but I can no longer feel the motivation of that relinquishment. Those feelings are long forgotten. Now all I can ask is, what kind of a mother am I to care for three of my children and not all four? What kind of a mother am I to have given up my child in the first place?

And is my love for my "lost sheep" starting to overshadow my love for those safely within my fold?

Remembering back to February 26, 1979

The entire maternity ward buzzed. Nurses and other patients chattered about the total eclipse of the sun that would happen that morning. Nurses passed out protective films to women so they could watch this natural phenomenon without damaging their sight, while I sat and held two day old Sarah in my hospital bed next to the window. An eclipse of the sun held no fascination for me, it being far outshone by the baby I cuddled.

Later that afternoon, long after the eclipse, Bob came to visit. He settled in a chair by my bed as I gave Sarah her bottle. In low murmurs we agreed how beautiful she was, how deeply I loved her. How it was going to break my heart not to see her grow up. For some reason we didn't talk about her prospective adoptive parents. And I never asked. I didn't think I could. Who was I, but a silly girl who'd been irresponsible? My child deserved better, and if I really loved her...if I really loved her...?

Hot tears streamed down my face and splashed onto Sarah's little face. Bob leaned over in his chair closer to my hospital bed. "She's your baby, Christine," he said quietly. "She's your little girl. You can keep her if you want to."

I gulped down a draught of air as if I'd been drowning. She was my baby. My child. I wanted to keep her with all my heart. I'd wanted to keep her since the moment I found out I was pregnant. All through the lonely months of pregnancy as I'd prayed about adoption, chosen a prospective couple, the cry of my heart tolled inside me, *I want to keep my baby.*

Bubbles fizzed inside Sarah's bottle as she drank her formula. Her deep blue gaze latched on mine. She trusted me to do the best for her. After all, that's what mothers did.

As Bob sat at my bedside, the picture emerged in my mind of that faceless, nameless couple that I'd chosen for her parents. I assumed Bob had phoned to tell them he had a baby for them. I imagined, at this moment, the two of them rushing out to a department store, buying a stroller, a crib, all the things a baby would need. My vision blurred. With my shoulder I tried to wipe tears from my face, but they fell. Sarah's blanket soaked them up. I couldn't bear to break the hearts of this man and this woman. They were expecting a baby. My baby.

And there'd been the eclipse this morning. Was I naïve to think that God used a natural phenomenon to encourage me to stay the course? To not retreat from this huge step of faith. All these long months spent praying on my knees, I'd mulled over the image of Abraham trudging up that hill to give Isaac up to God. Just like Abraham—when God returned his son to him within the context of their unique story—I felt a parallel to mine and Sarah's story. That if I sacrificed Sarah through adoption, God would bring us together again one day. That he'd reserve some kind of special birth mom/ birth daughter relationship for us. That promise had filtered into my soul from the night I was sure Jesus stood in my living room and said, "Trust me." And in my bones rested the surety that one day God would use our story to help others.

I struggled to get the words out. "No, I can't keep her."

Bob softened his voice further. "What about you, Christine? Will you forgive yourself for giving her up?"

My voice weakened to a whisper as I clutched Sarah closer. "I want her to have what I never had, a daddy as well as a mommy. It would be harder for me to forgive myself if…if I did keep her."

As Sarah snoozed in her bassinette beside my bed that night I wrote in my journal:

> Every time I put her down to sleep, she whimpers and cries like a little bird. I rock her, and she snuggles in warm and soft. Her little head lies against my shoulder, her tiny breaths against my neck. I kiss the softness of her forehead and tuck her legs against my body.

> There's so little time. I tell her how much I love her. To love and obey her new parents, to be a good girl. I tell her I will never stop loving her, never stop thinking about her. I tell her about Jesus dying on the cross for her, that if we never meet on this earth again, I will wait for her in heaven. I ask her to try to remember me. The only thing that gives me hope is that I am just like Hannah. I'm giving my child to the Lord. For her whole life she will be given over to the Lord.

The next day my mother arrived on the ward as patients finished their breakfast. Other mothers dawdled over their meal. In due course they'd get dressed, husbands and family would gather the new mother's belongings, and they'd go home together, taking their babies with them. They had their baby's childhood to look forward to. I had no such luxury. Only a few hours.

Instead my mother and I cherished every moment as we fed Sarah her bottle, burped her, and simply held her, trying to store up memories to last a lifetime. Sarah's bright blue eyes fixed on mine as I shampooed her hair and she moved her rose petal mouth in a tiny moue. Together my mum and I dried her and dressed her in the special outfit my mother had bought for her in the most expensive baby shop in Vancouver.

As my mother held Sarah for a while, I took out the little Bible I'd bought for her and quickly skimmed the pages, searching for a verse or two that would secretly convey what I wanted. For some reason I thought I'd not be allowed to send a letter. Then my eye spotted two passages from Psalms 127 and 128. "Lo, children are an heritage of the Lord: and the fruit of the womb is his reward." And, "Yea, thou shalt see thy children's children" (KJV). I quickly underlined both verses and sat back against the pillows.

There...it was done. *Oh dear Lord, help them to understand when they flip through this small white bible and see these verses underlined, help them understand my secret request, the longing of my heart that I want to see them and Sarah one day when she is grown.* I placed the white Bible on top of the box of layette items I'd put together for Sarah.

The wretched time passed too fast. When Bob and his wife Beverly arrived, they spoke softly so as not to waken Sarah. Their smiles held a tinge of sadness on this day of contradiction. Soon this baby would go to her new parents—an occasion to rejoice—and one mother would be left with empty arms, childless—an immeasurable loss.

Though my denomination practices baptism on individuals who can verbally state their faith in Christ, I asked Bob to perform an infant baptism for Sarah. This important and treasured Christian sacrament was more for me than her. I knew in my heart her parents would lead her to faith in the Lord as she grew, but I yearned to share a sacred moment with her now.

In the head nurse's office, Bob lifted Sarah, supporting her body and head in his two hands. Beverly held a small jug of warm water, and my mother lifted a basin beneath Sarah's head.

"I baptize you, Sarah, in the name of the Father, the Son, and Holy Ghost. I pray the Lord will bless you from the top of your head to the tips of your toes; that you will be a good daughter to your new parents and grow up to be a godly woman." Bob also prayed that God would comfort and strengthen me.

Sarah didn't cry, but slept peacefully as Bob took the jug and poured a trickle of warm water over her head. My mother caught the water in the basin.

I dried Sarah's hair, fluffing the golden down. Carefully, Mum helped me tuck my baby's tight little arms, so much like the folded wings of a bird, into her soft pink sweater. Lifting the hood over her head, I tied the strings, bringing together the two pink woolen pompoms under her tiny chin.

Nearby, the head nurse, with compassion straining her eyes, waited to snip off the hospital ID bracelets, those around my wrist and the match from around Sarah's baby ankle. Bob took care of some paperwork while I clasped Sarah close and watched her sleep.

A long time later Bob gently touched my arm and whispered, "Are you ready, Christine?"

I placed Sarah on the bassinette so my mother could help me wrap her in the two new lacey shawls, one white, one pink.

Then I clutched Sarah close to say goodbye and breathed a prayer. "Please remember me."

I stepped back, allowing the nurse to take over. She wrapped Sarah tighter in her shawls and started down the hall. Bob picked up the box of things I'd wrapped in pink paper for Sarah, including the small white Bible with the secret verses underlined.

Bob, Beverly, and the nurse carrying Sarah made their way down the hall to the elevators. My mother and I followed but remained at the doors as the other three, with Sarah, stepped into the elevator.

The cold, gray, steel elevator doors closed between my child and me, and I dropped to the floor, sobbing soundlessly. My mother caught and held me.

From The Fraser Valley, Canada, the Adoption of Sarah
"Life Became a Whirlwind"
By adoptive mother Anne VandenBos

Hans and I went to Bob's apartment at Trinity Western University to get Sarah. To us, she was a gift straight from heaven. When I held her in my arms, she looked right at me. She was so alert for being only four days old. Tears of joy wet my face. I could hardly wait to get home with our precious daughter.

All I could say was, "Thank you, Jesus. Thank you, Jesus," over and over again.

It was such a privilege to be chosen as her parents. We didn't know how many profiles the birth mom had to choose from, but we knew she had choices without knowing the applicants' names. I am convinced that the Holy Spirit led her to choose us to raise her child in the ways of the Lord.

Hans and I were so grateful to the Lord for such a healthy baby. She was the blue-eyed blond that so many adoptive parents want. It is such a blessing to be able to raise a child from infancy, and I had no fear of taking care of a baby because I already had twelve nieces and nephews. We were willing to adopt older children, but having a baby was the desire of our hearts.

Life became a whirlwind for us, and I was excited beyond belief. I found myself doing senseless things like putting my coffee into the fridge to warm it up, instead of the microwave, or spraying hairspray instead of deodorant under my arms.

Hans thought Sarah was perfect. He loved to sit by her crib and watch her sleep. The first Sunday she was in the church nursery, he went to pick her up and at lunchtime, he told my mom that she was the most beautiful baby in the nursery.

Our parents and family were delighted for us, showering us with love. They accepted Sarah into our family circle with open arms and praise to God for answered prayers.

7

Relinquishment

Christine, March 1999

From the moment I received Anne's letter, that floating sensation has carried me, a feather on the breeze, the same as when David and I told Lana about Sarah. With the reunion planned for Saturday, my heart beats untethered. I'm soaring free. I grin and constantly murmur quiet thanks to God as I go about my day. My joy isn't all about Sarah though. I'm on top of the world that Lana is going on the church's youth mission trip to Mexico. God answered my prayers for her too. I'm so proud of my girl for her desire to help build a small medical clinic there.

And the boys are doing great. As always, they're taking the disclosure of Sarah diametrically differently. Each in their own way tries to come to terms with this sudden change in how they perceive their family. After we told them about their new sister, Robert, the youngest—always the most demonstrative in his affection—cuddles up on the couch with me more frequently. At ten, his questions astound me—questions not about Sarah, or how I had a baby back then and wasn't married, but about how I'm feeling about meeting Sarah.

Kyle, however, sidles up to me the day before the reunion. Normally he'd be out in the garage tinkering with something, but today he lingers in the kitchen as I clean up after lunch. I recognize that loitering stance. I also know that slightly gruff expression he wears. From a toddler, that frown has covered up one big marshmallow heart. Clamping my lower lip between my teeth and drawing in a deep breath, I gently nudge Kyle to sit down with me at the kitchen table. "No matter what happens when I meet Sarah tomorrow, it will make no difference to how I feel about you."

He glances up, a frown pulling his brows together.

I go on. "As much as I love Sarah, and though she was my child, she and I can never share the same bond that I've had with you since you were a baby. You're my kid."

His frown starts to melt, but he remains so very still.

I lean a little closer. "I want you to know that I really love Sarah, and it hurt me so much to give her up, but I lost the original relationship with her, and I've come to accept that." I hide my inner twinge that this isn't completely true.

An openness grows on his usually intense face. How strange that it seems to please him that I love Sarah. As if that's an important building block, although he's not exactly sure where that block fits. Even I can't fit the blocks of my own heart together, and the constant strain is fast becoming a tide I can't swim against.

"Kyle"—I measure my words—"any future relationship I might have with Sarah will be different and unique for all of us. Hopefully, it'll be more like the relationship we have with Aunt Sherry." How is it I can speak so sensibly to my children, the right nurturing tone, when in my private thoughts I flounder, hoping for a natural bond with my firstborn? But I'm pleased when Kyle nods as he thinks about my brother's wife.

"Remember?" I prompt. "We didn't know Sherry until Uncle Stephen introduced her to us. Now she's part of the family. I really hope something like that happens between us and Sarah. A new relative."

Kyle gives me another short nod.

"Are you okay with all this, sweetheart?" I pray silently, *Please be okay. Please be okay.*

"Yeah, Mom." No smile, but his frown and that intense look melt somewhat. He leaves me to go out to the garage. He'll continue to think this over as he takes something apart and puts it back together again. That's Kyle's gift, the way he looks at the world. His mechanical mind strives to understand things by dismantling and reassembling gears and mechanisms. He'll work through his feelings about Sarah and me in a similar manner. Surely he'll see the importance of that building block and realize the fact that I have never stopped loving Sarah only reaffirms the love I have for him. Because mothers never stop loving. Mothers never forget.

Last night in my devotions I read John 16:19-21 where Jesus says, "In a little while you will see me no more, and then after a little while you will see me...your grief will turn to joy. A woman giving birth to a child has pain because her time has come; but when her baby is born she forgets the anguish."

My mind repeats those words like a catechism, and my hands tremble as I dress for the reunion today. The heartache is over. In a few hours I'll see my firstborn. All my prayers will be answered.

David and I hug the kids as we leave the house early. I tell them to be prepared for anything, that if all goes well, who knows—maybe we'll swing by later in the afternoon, bringing Sarah and her family with us. The sun-filled air fizzes like champagne as David drives the long way from Maple Ridge to Surrey, hugging the Fraser River. No matter how hard he tries, his sweet attempt to calm me can't replace a placid stream for the deep torrent racing beneath my surface.

We stop at a florist to pick out four pink carnations—three long-stemmed—one for Sarah's mom, one for her future mother-in-law, one for Sarah herself, and a boutonniere for Bob.

The closer we get to Surrey, the more my hands shake. The expensive, light-blue linen skirt I bought for the occasion is already wrinkled. My new scarf chokes me. Normally I never wear scarves, but today I want to project the image that I'm a really nice mother. A completely together, ordinary but confident, Proverbs 31 woman who loves all her kids. Even if she gave up one of them.

As my fingers loosen the scarf, they brush the fine heart-shaped gold locket Jim gave me so long ago—and that's been in my jewelry box and never worn again once I met David. At least this act of love on her birth father's part will accompany Sarah and me today. Pink flowers. Gold locket. The gifts for Sarah that Lana and Robert helped me wrap.

I'm happy. Gloriously, over the moon happy. And scared to death.

What if I'm a disappointment? Sarah's so pretty, she and her parents might be expecting some beauty of a birth mother, which I am not. Plus, her mom's a teacher—I'm a bank teller. Sarah's studying to be a nurse—I only had two years of college. And I was the one to get pregnant out of wedlock.

But no. I've prayed for twenty years. God has this all under control.

When David and I arrive at Bob's office, our gazes glide over the parking lot. Which car might be Sarah's, her fiancé's, or her parents'?

We climb the stairs up one flight, and I'm sure I've memorized each and every step, every moment crystalized forever. Numb with nerves, so cold, I shake. "Breathe," I tell myself on a tight swallow. "Keep breathing."

At the end of the hall, Bob holds the door open and ushers us through his waiting room to his office. His twinkling grin says it all as he invites us to sit. "How you doing, Chris?"

"Never been so scared in my life." How can I express to him this quaking in my very being?

He just chuckles, and then his phone rings. His eyes meet mine as he talks with someone. When he hangs up he says, "That was Sarah. They're on their way. About another twenty minutes."

Twenty more minutes. I have to keep breathing though my heart pounds so strongly I'm sure it will cease. Less than half an hour. *But what if they don't like me? Why should they like me? I don't even like me.*

Bob's smile diminishes a little. "Christine, I know you were hoping that Sarah's mom and dad would be here today."

"Yes," I say on a suspended breath. Something deep within me shudders.

"I've been on the phone to Hans and Anne quite a bit, trying to encourage them to come today. Don't take this the wrong way, but they're not coming. They're...well they're quite upset...finding the reunion very hard emotionally. Sarah's dad especially doesn't understand why you want to meet Sarah...or them."

My heart stops. The day I've prayed for all these years, and they're upset...finding it...hard? They don't understand? The world tilts on its axis. I'm falling off, into the ether, untethered to float forever. I can't breathe.

David's hand touches my knee. "Chris? Honey?" He's reaching

across from his chair to mine.

I turn slowly to lock gazes with my husband. Secure in his love, I gulp down some air. Bob and David peer at me where I'm still sitting upright on my chair. Have been all along. I manage to croak through a constricted throat. "I never wanted to hurt anyone." But my mind screams, *They don't want to meet me!* Why? All these years I thought they'd want to meet me as much as I wanted to meet them. And most of all—I gave them my child!

"I never wanted to hurt anyone," I repeat in a tight voice, and David winces with me.

"I know that," Bob softly affirms. He leans over to rest his elbows on his knees, the same way he did when he visited me in the hospital just two days after Sarah's birth. I recognize that piercing look, the one I'd seen all too frequently for a full year after the relinquishment when he counseled me over the loss of my daughter. "I know you, Christine. I know how you'll turn this around and beat yourself up. Give it time. Give them a chance. Let Sarah see the real you—the Christine we all know and love—and you'll win her over in no time. Eventually, maybe even her parents."

The real me. Oh dear God.

Bob leans back in his chair with a grin. "Besides, your daughter's on her way. And her fiancé."

I nod, working hard to control my trembling. I'll do my best. Can this be any harder than giving up my child? And Sarah, my precious daughter, I'll be seeing her in moments. Moments only. *But I want them too, Lord. As much as I want to see Sarah, I want them too. Dear Lord, I'm so drained already, as though I could sleep a thousand years in the soft mud beneath this tumultuous river of emotion.*

My tired pulse jumps to overdrive again when the intercom buzzes. Bob answers it, and then he stands with David and me, joining all of our hands together. As Bob prays, I imagine Sarah entering the same foyer downstairs. I picture her coming up the one flight. Does she take the elevator or the stairs like me? Is she now walking down that long hallway? "Breathe," I tell myself. "Breathe."

Bob leaves David and me to go out to his waiting room. A minute later he returns to his office and leads us into the overly bright waiting room.

Everything recedes. No walls, paintings, no office furniture. A tall, slender girl on the brink of womanhood stands up to meet me. Her long hair that I always knew would be blond softly frames her face and rests on her shoulders. Like mine used to do. The brightness of the lights hurt my eyes as though I'm standing within a sun-filled cloud. I know her. But no...I don't know her. Though I've seen photos of her, she's different today. Animated. More beautiful. A real person. My daughter? *And...yet...I feel no connection. Lord, how can that be? Oh dear God, what's wrong here?* Mentally, I reach for the emotional tether of David, who I sense is standing behind me.

But David, Bob, and the young man at the periphery of my vision—Mark—all vanish again. I lock on to what facts I can quickly gather about Sarah. She's lightening her dark blond hair like I do. She inherited her slenderness from me. Sarah and I attempt a smile at each other. Hers comes across a little wobbly, unsure, as I know mine must be too.

"Sarah, is it you?" I feel stupid, not knowing what else to say.

"Yes, I'm Sarah." Her voice sounds confident, but behind it I catch a hint of nervousness, like an intelligent student standing at the podium practicing composure.

For so long I've imagined this moment, that it would be like the movies. I thought we'd fall into each other's arms, cry, laugh through tears. Only the sense that I'm moving in slow motion—like film slides clicking past—resembles the movies. I thought we'd feel an instant bond. I've been counting on that bond. Counting on a natural love to waft from Sarah as I hope mine wafts toward her. But it doesn't. I try to remind myself of the words I spoke to Kyle, that a relationship with Sarah will be different.

We embrace. My brain hammers out, *I don't know you.* A hundred thoughts tumble. She's not crying, but neither am I. She's thinner than her pictures portrayed. Is she losing weight in college like I did? She looks more like Jim than me. *Dear God, I don't know her. I should know her.* Panic closes my throat, and I wish I could stop shaking and stop babbling nonsense. As if I'm standing outside myself, I can hear myself making small talk after our initial hello. *Please, dear Lord, help me, help us both.*

Sarah hands me a huge bouquet of pink carnations. At any other time I'd gush over the flowers, but not today. Forgetting for now the ones I'd brought, I give these a cursory glance and practically shove them at David to take care of. Now that I'm seeing her, I no longer want the dream of those mysterious flowers. I want my daughter. Still...she'd paid close attention to my long letter. Missed no detail. Is she a deep thinker like I am, one who tries to see far beneath the surface?

Frankly, we stare at each other. I drink in her every detail, the casual jeans and sweater, her comfortable shoes. And she's so pretty, my heart cries. Lana's pretty too, looking more like David than me, but I've always hoped Sarah would resemble me, so that we'd know each other, the same way we could look in a mirror and recognize our own reflections. But Sarah's face holds a lot of Jim's fine features. As her birth mother, physically I must be a disappointment.

When our eyes meet she doesn't seem confused like me, but her wobbly smile grows comforting. I take strength from that smile even though I feel it comes from an emotional distance, like a nurse to a suffering patient.

This is worse than meeting complete strangers. Both of us shy, polite. Oh so terribly polite. I can see plainly that she's putting up a protective barrier, while I fight with myself to hold back what has to be gushing need. But is it possible that Sarah is able to cover up her vulnerability like I can? Though I hope it doesn't show, only five minutes into our reunion I want to bolt for the door. Because it's so heart-rendingly-clear that what I've dreamed of is going to be a lot harder to attain than I anticipated. And I don't have the strength for a new set of emotional hurdles.

My energy is all but gone, as if I've just run a marathon, and we've barely gotten past hello. It's a relief when Sarah introduces her fiancé Mark, who's also studying to become a nurse. Mark, David, and Bob lend their warm, relaxed personalities to the reunion, while I'm shaking so hard I think my bones will snap. Bob, smiling, prepares to leave, and my panic spikes. I can't do this on my own, even if I do have David here. There's not enough beauty in my person to attract Sarah like Bob believes I can. No, I need Bob's charm to help me woo her.

Instead I simply ask, "Do you have your boutonniere, Bob?"

With an encouraging smile he lifts the pink carnation and informs me he'll wear it at his speaking engagement later today. Then he leaves.

To cover the awkward silence, I give Sarah the gifts I've brought for her—the small pink pearl on a fine gold chain and the little porcelain treasure chest that contains our hospital ID bracelets from when she was born. A slight chink shows in the barrier Sarah has erected. She flashes a quirky smile on her wide, tender mouth as she opens up and immediately clasps the pink pearl necklace around her neck. For the first time I sense a side to her that wants to laugh and have fun, but I feel it plainly—she's holding herself back from me. Her fingers gently shift the plastic ID bracelets inside the treasure box, and this leap into her past seems to lift a layer of that reservation.

"You look a lot like your birth father," I say, now that some strength has returned to my voice.

"Do I?" Again she smiles and with a tiny bit of trepidation says, "To start with, I'd like to know about you."

Sarah listens intently to everything I say with a reverence that awes me. I can see her storing away all I share as missing pieces to the puzzle of her background. We discover we like a lot of the same literature: C. S. Lewis and Jane Austen. She wants to know more about her Irish heritage. She too loves to dance and doesn't seem to have an athletic bone in her body. She's working her way through university, like I worked through my college years. "One of my jobs is scooping ice cream at the mall in Abbotsford," she adds.

I practically jump out of the chair. "I used to scoop ice cream too, working through high school and then college."

It doesn't take long to discover that we both adore cats.

David chimes in, "Boy, did that one ever come through the genes."

From her mom's letter I know that Sarah is in the second year of her degree, and I ask her to tell me about her nursing.

Her face lights from within. The polite, professional stranger disappears. Sarah inches forward on the edge of her chair, sparkling as she talks about serving as a nurse on the mission field one day. She's already been on a few short mission trips as a teenager. "Ever since I was a little girl I've wanted to be a missionary nurse. I'm really hoping that's God's plan for my life."

Pride fills my voice as I tell her that Lana is going on her first mission trip this summer, and Sarah gives a quiet smile. Is she storing all these facts and similarities away? I hope so.

Then Sarah pulls out a box of photo albums she's brought. I hunger to see her years of growing up. But as the photos whiz past—showing Sarah a few days after I relinquished her, being held in the arms of grandparents, uncles and aunts, learning to walk, hugging her baby twin brothers, going on camping trips, embracing her dad, standing and smiling beside her mom, going out with Mark—we talk and talk and talk, but the old tide of sadness laps constantly at my heart.

While our conversation over the photo albums flies at the speed of light, I don't know whether to feel curious or jealous that I missed every one of her milestones, especially as I linger over the photos of Anne and Hans. An odd mix of pain and love swirls within me. They have been such an integral part of my heart, my very being too, not just Sarah's. I gave my child to them. From looking at the adult Sarah—her kindness, her deep-seated compassion for a hurting world—to her wonderful childhood flowing past in photos, I know God has answered all my prayers for her. Hans and Anne have been the selfless, devoted parents I knew they would be all those years ago when I chose them from a portfolio.

I feel Sarah's gaze on me as I slow over the photos of her parents. She speaks softly. "They loved me unconditionally." Her voice dips lower. "I never felt abandoned like some adopted kids feel. From my earliest memory my mom told me that you gave me up out of sacrifice and love."

A wave of joy crashes with an undercurrent of loss. I struggle for control. *Thank you, Anne, oh thank you.* But still, jealousy eddies through me. If only...if only...if only what? That I could have been there all those years? Would an open adoption have made any of this easier?

All the while looking through the photo albums, Mark has also talked, pointing out things Sarah might have missed. Her features soften as she looks up at him, and though she doesn't move, I sense her spirit nestle against him, thankful for his help. From the start, the combined strength and sweetness of David and Mark are my and Sarah's respective ports of calm.

"It must have been so hard for you," Mark says, his eyes filling with sympathy. Sarah's fiancé acknowledges the sadness I try to hide, as if he is freer to do so than she is. There is so much in her life that I'm not privy to—perhaps never will be privy to—so that I cannot see behind her protective barrier. All I sense right now is her caution.

With the turning of each page, I have no way of gauging Sarah's feelings while I fear my face shows more and more of my neediness. With what Bob told me, I know she must be protecting her mom and dad. And with each photo, it becomes increasingly clear that the bond I've carried in my heart for Sarah never existed for her. This is her life. This is her family. In a flash of self-protection I inwardly shout, *I'm only the answer to some questions, the missing piece to her DNA puzzle, not a part of her family, not needed.*

I listen to Sarah chatting about the wonderful childhood she's had. Half my brain filters this with common sense. Of course she wants to reassure me that I made the right decision for her. Sarah and her brothers feel a special badge of honor at being adopted. If this was any of my friends with their adopted children I'd be one of the first to trumpet the rightness of it. Of course they should be proud of how God put their family together.

But for me, today, I keep waiting at the end of everything Sarah says, hoping for just one word that she wishes...that she wishes... I have no idea how to phrase what I want to hear from her. That she wants me in her life?

Thank God there's not one single ounce of rejection in her soul. Sarah's cup of love has been filled to the brim and overflows. Most of all, she's had the loving daddy I never did, just like Lana, Kyle, and Robert have with David.

I should be weeping with joy. Should be delirious with happiness. But after this, will Sarah close the photo albums, shake my hand, thank me for bringing her into the world, and then walk out of my life? *Oh dear God, no, please no.* Aside from the few close moments when I think I'm seeing the real her, we're two highly functioning mechanisms, circling each other, trying to figure out where—or if—this gear or that gear should be connected. Like something Kyle would concoct in our garage.

I'm afraid to lay my question on the table. "Do you think you'd like to see us again?" I hold my breath.

"Yes," she says slowly. "But probably not until after the wedding. With exams and preparations for the wedding, it's a bit crazy." Her protective barrier has gone up again. Thoughts flutter behind her eyes. She's got to be more vulnerable than she projects. "But please come to the wedding ceremony," she quickly adds. "It's a big church, and we'd love to have it filled. Why, just the other day I said to my future mother-in-law that the only person not coming to my wedding is my birth mother."

I too am more vulnerable than I can show. My brain acknowledges the fact that Sarah can't invite me as the honored guest I so long to be…that I've fantasied about over the years. Being old-fashioned, stubborn Irish, I clamp on to the fact that she didn't say anything about being invited to the reception. Only to the ceremony. Bewildered, shocked, I press on, dreading the answer I know is coming. "Do you think your parents would ever like to meet…us?"

Again a cloud passes behind her eyes. Her loyalty is to her parents, as it should be, I argue mentally. Though in the slight way Sarah hunches forward, her kindness stretches across the few feet between our chairs, her unspoken attempt to convey how hard the reunion is on her parents, that it's an unexpected trauma at the same time they're adjusting to her leaving their family to get married.

All along Mark has been sitting beside her. Although they don't overtly touch, his protective support of Sarah is palpable. And yet, while I know without being told that he will do anything to shield Sarah—even from me—his compassion is there for me too, an almost tangible thing. At the same time, I feel David's hand lightly caressing my back, my slim link to wholeness.

Looking into Sarah's face—surrounded by blond hair like mine, her mouth like Jim's, the shape of her eyes like Jim's but with my blue-gray color—I try to understand what's behind her words. Why should it be difficult? Silently I shout to God, *We all love Sarah. We all have roles in her life. Anne and Hans are her parents. I'm her birth mother. Isn't there a place for a birth mother? Like an extra aunt? A cousin? Dear God, even just a crummy friend of the family.*

That tidal wave of maternal yearning pulls me out deeper and deeper. As much as I want to cry right now, I stuff it down. On the outside I smile when Sarah and I decide we don't want the day to end just yet, and they agree to come out to the house to meet the kids.

As David and I rush into our home while Mark and Sarah park their car, we prepare our three kids, but Kyle slips upstairs. Even with gentle encouragement from David, he doesn't want to come down to meet them. This I understand. I barely take a breath to consider the double standard. If it's okay for Kyle not to meet them, why isn't it okay for Sarah's parents to not meet me? From downstairs I silently bless Kyle with the space he needs and pray for his peace of mind, because having Sarah in the same room as Lana and Robert after all these years overwhelms me. These waves of loss and joy buffet me back and forth.

Because there she is—my tall, slender daughter, the same shape and height as Lana, with blond hair just like mine—walking around my living room. I catch her quiet smile as she studies the womanly details I've put into my home. Through this chink in her barrier I see a glimpse of the Sarah that Mark and her family know so well. She stops to admire the hydrangeas I dried and arranged on top of my china cabinet. "Did these come from your garden?" she asks, her brows going high.

"Yes, I love to garden." I start to tell her about my favorite flowers and of my misadventures trying to grow vegetables. Something warms within me that this aspect of me, a grower of flowers, intrigues her—not the "me" as her birth mom, but just me.

Lana and Robert are clearly nervous yet excited, perching on two ends of the couch flanking me in the middle. Their easy friendliness shows that they want to get to know Sarah and Mark, who sit on the loveseat. David makes tea in the kitchen. Once again photo albums, both Sarah's and ours this time, are hauled out, and lives compared. I greedily stash away every similarity, such as the fact that Sarah and Lana agree that Jane Austen is the best.

"I can't get along without frequent doses of Lizzy and Mr. Darcy," Lana quips.

"Which is your favorite Austen novel?" Sarah asks.

Lana's eyes shine. "Probably *Persuasion.* I love second chances at love."

"*Persuasion*'s my favorite too," I agree.

"And your favorite?" Lana asks Sarah.

Sarah leans back. "I think I like *Pride and Prejudice* best. I love

Lizzy's character, her spunk and strength. I also like how the story starts off with her and Darcy misjudging each other completely but eventually seeing past it."

There are plenty of DNA parallels—similar smiles, their long-legged figures, that hint of goofiness that I only get a peek at in Sarah, as though it's a vein of gold I must dig for. Yet with every sameness there are so many differences. With those few, slim glimpses into the real Sarah, I still feel that barrier. Her smile is so quiet, so polite.

The day wears on, and exhaustion reaches its peak for both Sarah and I, and I know that the little girl I've imagined all these years and loved was truly a phantom. Bob is so wrong. There's no way I can win Sarah's affections. There's no natural bond in Sarah to build upon.

As David, Lana, Robert, and I say good night to Mark and Sarah, with the vague promise that she'll send us the date and time for the wedding, we wave as they drive off. As my family disperses to the living room, I lay my head against the front door, and the sobs erupt. Not quietly this time, like I cried that day on the maternity ward floor as the cold gray, steel elevator doors closed—holding in my full despair. This time I howl. This time the swirling dark waters of loss sweep me fully out of my safe harbor, out to the depths.

All these years, have I truly understood the magnitude of my loss, understood what I did in giving up my child?

Remembering back to February 27, 1979

My mother and I took a taxi home to my apartment after we left the hospital. My sister Irene met us there. She'd moved in to share the apartment with me a few months earlier but had not wanted to be at the hospital when I gave up Sarah. Tight-lipped, Irene's every nuance clearly said, *We could have kept her. You didn't have to give her up. I'd have taken care of her.* And I loved my sister for the pain we shared in giving up Sarah.

A little later my mother and sister went out for groceries. Alone, I tried to rest. But as I slept my breasts filled with milk and ached. A phantom fluttered in my abdomen as if my baby still snoozed there. I kept hearing her cries. I pushed my face into my already damp pillow.

The buzzer to my apartment sounded, and I struggled to the door, feeling the pains of recent childbirth fully for the first time. A florist waited below. A few minutes later I opened my door to a girl who handed me a long white cardboard box. The card only said it was from an anonymous friend at my mother's workplace.

Inside the box lay an extravagant spring bouquet—blue and purple irises, red and yellow tulips, white daisies and baby's breath, all interspersed with long-stemmed, large pink carnations. As I arranged the flowers in a vase, I lifted one of the carnations and touched it to my nose, sniffing the delicate powdery fragrance. The tight, fluffy roundness of the blooms resembled the soft pink pompoms on the little sweater that I'd sent Sarah away in. I slumped to a chair.

The story of the biblical Hannah had given me the strength to give up Sarah. God had allowed Hannah to keep her baby until after she'd weaned him, but eventually her day of relinquishment arrived too. Hannah and her husband journeyed, taking baby Samuel to the house of the Lord at Shiloh. Hannah approached Eli. "Pardon me, my lord...I give him to the LORD. FOR HIS WHOLE LIFE HE WILL BE GIVEN OVER TO THE LORD."

No different than what I'd done for Sarah, but Hannah had the blessing of visiting her child once a year. As the year without Samuel passed, she would cut out material, maybe even dye or weave it herself, then create a brand new robe for Samuel. Every year at the same time as she relinquished him, she would travel to Shiloh and bring that new coat to her boy. No doubt she hugged him and kissed him and exclaimed with tears of joy over how much he'd grown in the last year.

I only had three days with my baby, but now I clutched that long-stemmed pink bloom close to my lips, as if it were the softness of her brow. This was my gift from God. His promise. The flowers seemed to silently encourage me. *God will not forget you, no more than you could ever forget your baby. He will not forget the desire of your heart to see your child again one day...you just have to wait until she is grown.*

From that day forward I prayed for Sarah and her mom and dad. They were a package deal that God had put together, and I loved them as much as I loved her.

From The Fraser Valley, Canada—The Adoption of Sarah
"Because of You"
By adoptive mother Anne VandenBos

The following is a poem written by Anne, enclosed in a letter that she wrote to Christine in the early '80s. She left it with Bob to deliver, but due to Christine and David moving several times, he never had a chance. Christine received this poem only after the reunion with Sarah in 1999.

Thank you for putting our daughter's life into the hands of the Lord.
We got her because of you.
Because of you...
our burden has been lifted.
Because of you...
we have a very special child
who is so precious to us.
Because of you...
Jesus has become more real to us
than we ever knew could be possible,
and best of all,
we've been able to tell others
how they, too, can know the Lord...
...because of you.

~ Anne VandenBos

8

Just Call Me *Mara*

Christine, March 27, 1999

Kyle comes downstairs at last, but as the kids hear me sobbing, the three of them stay in the living room out of the maelstrom of my unleashed emotions. David pulls me into the kitchen and holds me close. I've kept a lock on my disappointment all day, having hoped for so much more closeness than Sarah has been able to offer. Now it unleashes, a wounded tiger uncaged.

"I've prayed for twenty years," I yell at David as I pull away, "prayed for twenty years that God would prepare their hearts so that no one would feel hurt. And this is the best he could do! This... *this* is the biggest disappointment of my life!" I cry out, "and God knows I've had enough of them."

David takes hold of me again. I resist, but he holds tight while my mind fights to sift through the avalanche of my emotions. I want to get to know my beautiful birth daughter, but my dream lies at my feet like shattered glass. She is my daughter, but not my daughter. I'm not a part of her family, nor have Sarah or her parents ever considered such a thing. Her mom and dad don't even want to meet me.

To David's pain-filled face I shout, "I'm invited to the wedding ceremony! Not the reception, like a proper guest. Just to the church. To fill a pew!" I hate myself for being so angry with Sarah's parents, for taking Sarah's invitation, the only way she could phrase it at this time, and turn it into something mean. But my desire for so much more drowns out all common sense.

Finally I free myself from David's clasp and bang my fist on the countertop. "How can he be so cruel? How can he let my heart be smashed again? As usual I'm nothing to him."

I cringe, shame seeping through the bitterness streaming from my mouth. I want to run and hide from the sheer humiliation of making my kids in the living room feel shaken and embarrassed by my outburst. I loathe my lack of gratitude, my anger, my jealousy. But I can't help it. It hurts. *Oh God, it hurts.* I cry, hating myself, hating the world, hating God. This is all his fault. He could have done so much better. But why had I thought I'd be anywhere but on the bottom of God's list of priorities?

After a long while I look into my husband's eyes and see his disappointment in me. I know the kids have the same looks on their faces though I can't see them in the living room. Their silence berates me. They haven't even turned on the TV. Remembered strains of violin music from all those specials on adoption reunion mock me. It's me—not anyone else, but me who's the failure, as I've been a failure in my past. I'm the disappointment on this day. I'm the one who fails to understand.

For the thousandth time I ask myself if, on the night of Sarah's birth, I would have kept her if I'd known the full extent of my emotional pain. On this night of our reunion, my soul screams out, "Yes! Yes!" If only I could turn the clock back.

The fact that Sarah is no longer nineteen inches long, weighing six pounds fifteen ounces, doesn't matter to me. The fact that she's six inches taller than me and on the threshold of marriage makes no difference. Every atom in my body cries out that she is my child.

I can't convince myself to just be happy that I have three other children. Nor can I simply view it as the wonderful blessing of Sarah's life with her parents, end of story. As a society we learned a long time ago to not console a woman who loses a baby to miscarriage with the words that she may have another child. That kind of simplistic encouragement is not what a bereaved mother needs. One child cannot be replaced by another. Lana, Kyle, and Robert are the very beats of my heart for all eternity, but Sarah cannot be torn from the steady cadence of my pulse either.

I am a bereaved mother.

I've come back full circle to the grief I thought I'd dealt with twenty years before. Is the reunion doing something similar to Sarah's parents? Has my resurrection from the past reminded Hans and Anne that their daughter is not of their flesh and blood? Has the reunion brought back the ghost of their original infertility?

The phone rings. A moment later David tells me it's Bob calling. As I take the receiver, I stand dumb, listening. Somehow I manage to coherently return his greeting. Lifeless as a mannequin, I listen as he explains that my expectations are too high. I swallow through a raw throat. "So Sarah's parents are pretty upset?"

He pauses. "Yes. Anne cried with me over the phone today. Reminded me of you twenty years ago."

I look up at my kitchen ceiling as twin hot rivers flow down my cheeks, into my mouth, and I taste the salt.

"Christine," Bob softly says, "did you get the bouquets I left for you and Sarah at the office today?"

"Yeah," I answer slowly. My clouded gaze searches out the various bouquets that David has put in water and left on the kitchen table. While Sarah and Mark were here at the house I had no emotional reserves to fuss over flowers and forgot them. The long-stemmed pink carnations from Sarah and those from Bob's bunch are arranged in a vase. Sarah must have her matching bouquet in their car, with the single long-stemmed blooms I sent along for her mom and future mother-in-law.

Bob's voice pulls me back. "Did you see the single pink rose in the middle of each bouquet?"

I walk over to the flowers to take a closer look, and my voice comes out dull. "Yes...there it is."

Bob's silence on the other end of the phone somehow warms me. "Don't expect too much too soon," he says. "Give it time. I gave you and Sarah the rosebuds to symbolize a new beginning."

A new beginning. Not the end. Is it possible the Lord will treat my words of despair as dust blown on the wind? The venom that had bubbled up inside me now drains away. Sympathy for Anne and Hans washes in like a gentle tide. So too does sympathy for Sarah for having to endure such a tug-a-war of emotions in the midst of university studies and marriage preparations.

Our three kids have gone to bed, and David and I sit at the kitchen table and pray for Sarah and her mom and dad, that the Lord will take away all our fears, any jealousy, anger. We also pray that Mark and Sarah will feel no pressure. And I pray especially, "Thy will be done, Lord. Thy will be done."

But as the days and weeks pass, my journals fill with bitterness. "My heart is torn," I write. "I have the bond of maternal love still within me, even though Sarah and I are strangers. How do I start a relationship in which I've already invested twenty years of love and prayer? Am I to grieve my loss again and again that I am not

Sarah's mom for the rest of my life?"

I read over my journals from the Christmas before when the Book of Ruth gave me such inspiration in my search for Sarah. But I'm not satisfied like Ruth was at the end of her story. I feel more like Naomi when she hollers out in the middle of their book, in that same gut-wrenching tone as me, "Don't call me Naomi...Call me Mara, because the Almighty has made my life very bitter."

I can just see Naomi, her losses too deep to articulate into sensible speech, hurting, hurting, crashing to her knees in the dust, feeling the thud echo through her body. Her other fist curls into a solid ball, and she raises it to the air, shaking it under the very nose of God. "You did this! You the Almighty have treated me cruelly."

New beginning, Bob said. "Huh," I scoff. All this time, believing that God encouraged me to search for Sarah, I've been wrong. Those pink flowers I believed were mysterious little miracles over the years, I read that all wrong. I only saw what I wanted to see.

But I've been wrong not only about the search.

As the kids go off to school each day, and David to work, I huddle in my house alone, remembering those three days in the hospital in 1979, remembering the strong sense that God wanted me to give Sarah up for adoption. All those years ago, it wasn't me giving Sarah to her parents. Instead, God took my child from me.

Relinquishing Sarah to adoption was, I believed, better for her. And now the thought snakes in—*better for her, not just because she needed a father, but because you weren't good enough to be her mother.*

Remembering back to February 24, 1980

A year had passed since the night of Sarah's birth. Her first birthday fell on a Sunday, and I sat in church quietly waiting for the evening service to begin. From the first few weeks immediately after relinquishing Sarah, an elderly woman in this congregation, Mrs. Gemmell, had taken me under her wing. I'd shared my full story with her, and in her fussy old-lady-way she counseled me, "Best to keep it hidden, dear—hidden under the blood of the lamb." With my past failures behind me I wanted to walk the straight and narrow, even if that meant as straight and narrow as this eighty-year-old woman. If Mrs. Gemmell said keep it all a secret, then that's what I would do.

I'd struggled with my Christian faith in the past, and now I'd swung to the farthest extreme. My goal became any service for God—anything that would keep my thoughts on the good things, the pure things, things that inspired hope. Anything that would help me not hear my baby's phantom cries in the night. To help me not shrink with sadness every time I saw a mother push a baby stroller past me on the street. A few weeks earlier I even enrolled for an evening class at the Northwest Baptist College and Seminary. While an Exposition of the Book of Acts sounded boring, I longed for anything that would help me think of God and not of the baby I'd given up.

On the evening of Sarah's first birthday, I looked back on the year. For most of it, Eva Gemmell had kept me glued to her side, co-teaching Sunday school together, insisting I help her with the youth group at Collingwood Baptist. Tonight, as I sat quietly in the hard wooden pew waiting for the Sunday service to begin, some of those young people were coming in and taking their seats too.

So, too, did the man I'd met at the beginning of January, the first night of the class on Acts. I'd come straight from work, got off the bus into a flurry of snow, and darted into the college building.

Running a bit late, another set of footsteps on the staircase coming up behind me surprised me. As I'd reached for the door, a masculine hand reached it first and held it open for me. I'd looked back to see a slender, not-terribly-tall guy smiling at me. His blue eyes held me still—blue eyes under untidy dark hair that swept over his brows.

That was the night I'd met Dave Schmidtke. Since then he'd been helping out at our church, and I'd seen him several times a week at youth events. Lately we'd even been attending Wednesday night prayer meeting with all the old folks, listening to missionaries like the one from the Ramabai Mukti mission in India. Never in my life had I been so faithful at church, and it was hard to miss all the knowing looks cast our way from the seniors. But I told myself not to hope for too much. Even if David and I were seeing each other almost five times a week at church, we had yet to be out alone for so much as a coffee.

He too entered the church tonight, though he took a different pew from the one I sat in. But my mild disappointment couldn't compare to the loss I'd been trying to control all day.

Her first birthday. I'd thought about Sarah like I did every day. Today though, I'd imagined her sitting in a highchair, her mom and dad feeding her cake with laughter. She probably wore a special party dress, surrounded by other loving relatives. As for me, my mother had dropped by this afternoon and we'd quietly remembered Sarah's birthday together. Mum had brought some flowers to cheer me. But it was the church bulletin from this morning's service that had brought me the only real comfort.

This morning as I'd sat in church, I'd stared at the bulletin uncomprehendingly, the covers which were pre-printed and purchased by the church. The picture on the front of today's bulletin had been that of a baby girl, lying in a cradle surrounded by pink flowers. But there'd been no babies born in our small church lately.

After the morning service I'd searched out the church secretary and asked, "Why did you choose that cover for today's bulletin? Were there any babies born that I don't know about?"

"Oh I just liked it," she said with an unabashed grin. "No babies right now, but I thought it was such a pretty picture, I just wanted to use it for today."

As I now waited for the evening service to begin, I pulled out the bulletin again and held it, tracing the date. February 24, 1980. I touched the picture of the baby girl, golden down on her head, surrounded by pink flowers. *Thank you, Lord, for remembering her birthday with me.*

After the evening service ended, the small congregation filed out. David threaded his way through a group of young people down the aisle to my side. He held an envelope in his hand. "I got a little something for you. I noticed you were feeling a bit down this morning."

I took the card from him, and he shyly drifted back to the youth group. I went home to the apartment I shared with my sister. In privacy I opened David's card that had a picture of a flowering meadow on the front. Inside were the words, "Those who go out weeping, carrying seed to sow, will return with songs of joy, carrying sheaves with them."

From The Fraser Valley, Canada—The Adoption of Sarah

"Between Midnight and Dawn"

By adoptive mother Anne VandenBos

The long-lost letter from Anne to Christine that wasn't delivered until years later shortly before the reunion.

To my sister in the Lord who "has put gladness in my heart" through our Lord Jesus Christ. This letter is long overdue! I've wanted to write you ever since we got our dearest baby daughter, but I kept putting it off, knowing that I'd need a post-midnight time for the Lord and me to write without interruption. I also knew that many a tear would flow in writing you. It's just that my heart aches when I think of you giving away the precious life we so greatly desired, even though we knew your baby was created by God for his purposes (Psalm 119). To me, you have indeed sacrificed in following the will of God. It is the closest earthly comparison that I think can be made to Christ sacrificing his life. My continual prayer for you is that you will experience the joy of the Lord as his reward to you for following his will.

Recently Bob told me that you have married and are starting a family of your own. That news was certainly an answer to my prayers for your happiness and it eased the hurt that I felt regarding your sacrifice. "According to the purpose of him who worketh all things after the counsel of his own will" (Ephesians 1:11 KJV).

My husband and I wanted a family for a long time. Your baby was such a wonderful answer to prayer for us. "For this child I prayed; and the Lord hath given me my petition which I asked of him" (1 Samuel 1:27 KJV). Bob said that he had other couples who wanted a baby, but every time he prayed about a home for your baby, the Lord laid my husband and me on his heart. It really was a miracle because we never specified that we wanted a baby, only a child no matter the age, but we got the desire of our heart. "Now faith is the substance of things hoped for" (Hebrews 11:1 KJV).

We feel so fortunate in having such a healthy child. Since the first time we looked at our little girl, we couldn't help but think, "This is the Lord's doing; It is marvelous in our eyes" (Psalm 118:23 NASB).

Our pride and joy has been a special baby book for adopted children. It was given to us by a friend who is also adopted. We think it is so special that her biological father was adopted too. I have six friends who are adopted, so adoption is not totally uncommon in our family.

Sarah loves Sunday school. She runs in and kisses her teacher. She sings parts of "Jesus Loves Me" and "Running Over." She repeats prayers well, and when she prays all by herself, she whispers, "Thank you, Jesus. Thank you, Jesus." She likes to "read" the Bible you gave her. She often "reads" upside down, pointing at the words and saying, "Jesus...story."

One day Sarah came running into the kitchen calling out, "Water! Water! I need some water!"

So I gave her a glass of water and followed her to see what all the excitement was about. She went into her bedroom and proceeded to open her Bible and pour the water on it!

Needless to say I put an end to that, and fast. For

one thing, I wanted that lovely white Bible to be a keepsake, and it certainly wouldn't last long with that kind of treatment.

Sarah is such a delight to us. We very rarely get evening babysitters because we enjoy being with her so much. She's not perfect, but you'd have a hard time getting her dad to admit it. He only spanks her on rare occasions. It has to be something very serious, like writing with crayons all over the wall. She really loves her dad, and he thinks the world of her.

Thank you for your continued prayers for our child. She is so fortunate to have two mothers praying for her. There are three things I think are the hardest for Christians to learn.

1. Sacrificing our self-will and following the leading of the Holy Spirit in obedience to the will of God.
2. Forgiving those who hurt us.
3. Witnessing for the Lord on a regular basis.

As we experience and conquer these mountains, I believe we benefit more than we ever would have imagined possible, as our heavenly Father has intended, and our relationship to him cannot help but grow closer and more wonderful. So you see, you are already giant strides ahead of many Christians.

It's been said, "Give and the Lord shall reward thee." And you have certainly given from your heart, body, and soul. "For God is not unrighteous to forget your work and labour of love" (Hebrews 6:10 KJV). May the Lord bless you with his abundant joy. You deserve it and have earned it.

Well, the birds have been singing for some time now. Daylight has arrived. I have enjoyed my time with you and in the Word. "God forbid that I should sin... in ceasing to pray for you" (1 Samuel 12:23 KJV), and "remembering without ceasing your work of faith, and labour of love" (1 Thessalonians 1:3 KJV).

I love you,

Your sister in the Lord, "and so shall we ever be with the Lord" (1 Thessalonians 4:17 KJV).

9

Desert in Bloom

Christine, April 1999

I do not want to go to Sarah's wedding. Day after day I keep telling David that. Any continuance or development of a relationship with Sarah is going to cost me too much. Now I understand some of those birth moms who cannot meet their relinquished children.

But at a birth mother support group I attend one evening, my face has the decency to go hot with shame.

According to most adoption-reunion standards, Sarah's and my reunion is a grand success. Other birth moms or birth dads wait for years for a reunion, and after an uneasy meeting they wait and wait for a second meeting or even just a phone call. I have the verbal invitation to Sarah's wedding, and the door to future get-togethers is open as well—just a crack—but still open. That is, if I don't do something stupid to blow that tenuous seedling of a relationship.

But I'm still blazing angry with God. Other adoption reunions are much better than ours. Other triads come together just as I always envisioned with hugs and the easy weaving of birth and adoptive family. I pick up a publication at the support group on adoption reunions, and a chapter on negotiating the birth mother role makes me want to throw the book against the wall.

How cold, how clinical—negotiating the birth mother role, indeed.

Several days ago David took me out for coffee to cheer me up. His words still haunt my thoughts. "You're too impatient, Chris, to wait for the good things God has in store for you." He held my hands across the table. "Sarah's parents might be afraid to allow Sarah's birth mother into their world, afraid this will take something away from their relationship with her."

"Maybe," I demur. "But the way Sarah spoke of them, if anything I'd say they are one of the strongest, most confident, most in-love adoptive families I've ever heard of. No, I don't think that's it. I'm just not wanted in the equation."

Each day as the kids go off to school and David to work, I isolate myself in the house, crying, venting my emotions in my journals, repeating the same thing over and over in different wording. Strangely, even in my rage toward the Lord I seek comfort in my Bible. And I pray, but my prayers swing from faith—that God still has a plan—to outright childish tantrums. I suppose if I go to my family doctor he might prescribe something. Surely I'm going through some kind of breakdown. All I know is I don't feel like someone's mother but rather like a broken, forgotten child, curled up in a fetal position. Why do I ache to reconnect with my first daughter when I'm failing to properly attend the three children in my care?

Yet with all my sulks, Romans chapter 8 secures me, a tether as slender and strong as silk thread. "Our present sufferings are not worth comparing with the glory that will be revealed in us...the whole creation has been groaning as in the pains of childbirth...as we wait eagerly for our adoption to sonship." Despair and depression may be gripping me fast as quicksand, but that fine thread—a life-line—holds my head up from complete drowning while God's patience, a ray of love, frays the dark cloud of my emotions.

Still though, I do not want to attend the wedding set for the long weekend in May. "Nope!" I keep telling David. "There's no way I'm going to subject myself to further rejection."

"And what do you think Christ felt when he came to the world? Rejection from the very people he came to save," David retorts.

"Well I'm not God," I holler back. "I can't do this." I have to stay tough. If I yield to even the slightest wooing of God's voice and give in to attend Sarah's wedding, then he'll keep pressing me to keep on loving, keep on putting myself out there. I'll only get hurt again and again.

But David, too, won't let up. "Okay, so you're not invited to the wedding reception. Maybe God wants you to attend the ceremony in a spirit of meekness."

Meekness. The word chimes like a distant bell. I certainly can't be brave or strong, but meek, yeah...maybe I can be that.

My husband softens his voice. "Remember back to when you obeyed God's direction and gave her up all those years ago. Through that single act of meek surrender, God gave Sarah a beautiful childhood, gave her all you wanted to give her. Obey again, one more act of generosity on your part, and see what God can make of it."

His words barely reach me, but I stoically record them in my journal in capital letters along with the other guilt gouging at me. I never meant to neglect my kids. Physically I still manage to take care of them, do their laundry, cook their meals, *sort of* clean the house, but my failure scrapes.

Lana's graduation is the one sparkling event this year that I'm honestly looking forward to. But I'm still emotionally focused on Sarah. Shopping with Lana for her prom gown, though I never verbalize it, many of my thoughts are on Sarah. At times I even forget the boys. Briefly, to be sure, not so anyone will notice. Still, for even a moment to forget one's child is unforgiveable. I'm not sure who they're playing with, assuming it's the usual bunch of boys in the neighborhood. I have no clue what Lana's dreaming about. We talk a little about her going to college. She's getting ready for her mission trip, but she always seems to be over at her friends' houses. And they're not the friends who go to church.

Isn't this the very thing I blamed God for, and isn't this what my own dad did to me? I'm going about *my own* business, *my own* agenda, *my own* compulsions, and I'm failing my kids.

As the weeks pass, Lana's silence toward me speaks louder than anything. Each time I threaten to not attend Sarah's wedding, she scowls at me and leaves the room. I'm the one who lifted the veil and told her about her sister more than two years ago. I'm the one who prepared her heart for the reunion and a possible relationship with her birth sister. Now I'm the one who's slamming the door shut? A good mother doesn't offer a sweet morsel to their child then yank it out of their child's mouth.

Even in regard to Sarah, I flinch at my attitude. I'm sure she can feel my temper twenty miles away. Can she sense that I'm unwilling to wait for her to work out a comfortable relationship with me, one that will bless her and not put her in a pressure cooker?

Our friends Eric and Kathryn give constant encouragement. At their house one afternoon I complain as usual. "I don't know if I can accept a distant sort of relationship with Sarah. I don't want to place myself in another vulnerable position, offering myself and my love with the fear of never having it returned."

Over their kitchen table, Eric peers at me through his glasses. "You know, Chris, what you've just described is unconditional love." He phrases his words in the warmest of friendship, yet they sting nonetheless. Where is the sacrificial love I've claimed all these years to have for her? My so-called love for Sarah's parents failed at its first test when I was so angry with their inability to meet me.

After all these years, do I understand what true love really is? During these past years of search and reunion, has it all been about me? Am I putting my own self-preservation above that of my children? My heart aches with pity for the kids I'm raising. If I wasn't good enough to keep Sarah, maybe I'm not good enough to be a mother to Lana, Kyle, and Robert either.

Remembering back to October 1, 1981

David and I had met in January of 1980 and were married by November that year, but on the night he started to propose, I stopped him. "There's something you need to know first." And I told him about my relinquishment of Sarah.

After he took in the full story, his frown deepened, his eyes filled, and he hugged me close. "I'm so sorry, Chris. I'm so sorry I didn't get here in time."

Only a year. If only God had allowed David into my life a bit sooner, I'd not have had to give up Sarah. David would have made such a wonderful father for her. From our engagement on he loved her as much as I did. It was not meant to be, though. We both agreed. And I had the sweetest man on earth as my husband. The only disappointment in my marriage, although I loved his mother and siblings, was his dad had passed away two years before we met. I'd forgiven my own dad for his failure as a father, but I would have liked a caring father-in-law to fill that void.

That disappointment would ease soon too, though, and it would be David bringing much of that needed healing into my life at my lack of a father. Not for me directly, but because eleven months after our wedding our first child was about to enter the world.

All night long throughout my labor, in the same hospital that Sarah had been born two and a half years earlier, David never left my side. Down the hall my mother waited. The pains for this child, my second, though as physically hard as giving birth to Sarah, were so welcome. Oh so welcome. As the contractions deepened and quickened, the nurses wheeled me down to the birthing room. I clutched David's hand as he walked along beside my bed. "This time I get to keep my baby."

As God had blessed Hannah after she relinquished Samuel, he was blessing me after giving up Sarah.

That morning we named our beautiful brunette doll with eyes as blue as pansies Lana-Joy, for the unspeakable joy her birth brought us. The following year I would sit in the rocking chair and hold Lana tight, singing to her the pop song, "My Girl." As the years passed, God filled my empty arms twice again, in 1983 with Kyle and in 1988 with Robert. No mother could have been happier. And watching David be a dad to our own three kids brought much of the healing I needed in my life that starved for "Father."

Still, I prayed for Sarah and her parents every day.

As my children played in the snow in the winter, in the woods or the beach in summer, I imagined Sarah a few years older doing the same sorts of things. I imagined her riding her bike as my kids rode theirs. When Lana first got behind the wheel, I imagined Sarah already driving. And as Lana neared her graduation, I'd imagined Sarah in college.

The years inched by, and David and I, my mother too, remembered

Sarah's birthdays. The mysterious flowers around Sarah's birthday continued to arrive, those silly blooms that started on the day I got out of the hospital with that surprise spring bouquet. Most especially the pink carnations.

God had allowed Hannah to go to Shiloh each year and bring Samuel a new robe, and each year God never forgot me. There were always the pink flowers.

In February 1997 David caught me staring out the kitchen window. "You're thinking about her, aren't you?" he asked.

"How'd you know?"

"I always know when you're thinking of Sarah, especially when her birthday is only a few weeks away. You want to take our annual drive through Abbotsford and try to guess where she lives?"

I smiled. "Okay, and have coffee somewhere. Maybe she'll walk right past us and I'll recognize her."

"How old is she this year?"

I turned from the kitchen window to tidy up the dishes. "Eighteen."

"Almost an adult. Are you going to start looking for her, hon?" His eyes twinkled.

"You think I should?" I held my breath. "You think she'll want to meet me?"

His smile grew warmer. "Why wouldn't she want to meet you? You worry too much."

"I'm scared," I said as I filled the sink with soapy water. "The closer it gets to her nineteenth birthday, the more I feel like a ticking time bomb. And the ticks are speeding up."

A frown knit his brow. "I know you're scared, Chris. Believe me, I know. All I can say is, God's been pretty good to you all these years. Trust him. He'll show you the way, and the when."

From The Fraser Valley, Canada—The Adoption of Sarah
"God's Perfect Timing"
by adoptive mother Anne VandenBos

In the late 1960s my husband and I were attending Johnston Heights Evangelical Free Church. One Sunday we noticed a mention in the bulletin of a Christian adoption agency in Seattle, called Burden Bearers. I began praying that Burden Bearers would open a branch in Canada. Ten years later, my prayers were answered. My husband Hans and I adopted the second baby available at Burden Bearers.

Our adoption of baby Sarah was "closed." The birth mother, Christine, didn't know our names; she only knew whatever our counsellor, Bob, chose to tell her. At the time of the adoption, Christine knew we couldn't have children, that we were practicing Christians, and that we were secure in our marriage. She had other families to choose from but felt led to choose us as Sarah's adoptive parent. Bob made it very clear to us that Christine wanted Sarah to know that she had wanted to keep her but decided it would be better for her to be raised by a mother and a father.

We received Sarah when she was four days old. From a very young age, I talked to Sarah about her adoption. We believed the longer we waited to tell her that she was adopted, the harder it would be to do it and the higher the risk of her finding out from a cousin or other family member. Also, if we told her about the adoption when she was older, she might be angry or wonder why we had lied to her for so long.

When Sarah was two years old, Bob, our adoption counsellor, was at a Sunday evening fellowship at our church. I overheard him talking to a group of people about a set of twins who needed to be adopted. On the way home from the service, I told my husband about it, and we agreed to submit our names as candidates to adopt the twins.

In the weeks to follow, we waited anxiously for any news from Bob. Two months later, we were told that the birth mother of the twins had chosen us! The twins were due on July 10, so there was barely enough time to move Sarah out of her crib into a big bed of her own—but there were enough days to share the excitement with Sarah that God was giving her twin brothers.

On the morning of July 9th, I fell to my knees in prayer. Sarah came and asked me what was wrong. I told her I felt we should pray for the twins' birth mother. When Bob phoned to tell me that the twins had arrived, he said there had been some difficulty with the birth of the second baby—ten minutes after his brother—but it was all over. The birth mom and babies were fine. The time of the twins' birth was at the exact time that I had fallen to my knees to pray.

Sarah loved her brothers from the very beginning, and we made a conscious effort to include her in their care. Whenever I would take the children shopping, people would ask questions such as, "Are they twins? What are their names? How old are they?" I would answer, and take care to include Sarah by saying, "And this is their two-year-old sister, Sarah." Sarah even had her own driver's license to push the twins' stroller while I pushed the cart when we went grocery shopping. She was totally capable of answering the common questions.

We made an effort to talk to Sarah, Matthew, and Luke about each of their individual adoption stories, because we wanted them to be proud of their history and thankful to God for the way he had brought our family together. If the topic ever came up at school, they were equipped to answer questions from the other children. I made personalized storybooks that became favorites of theirs because "Sarah," "Matthew," and "Luke" were the main characters.

When Sarah was a pre-teen, she asked some questions about her birth mother, and I shared with her and the twins all of the statistics that Burden Bearers had given us at the time of their adoptions. Although the boys hadn't asked any questions themselves, I also gave each of them a copy of their birth family's history. Sarah was surprised that there was so much information available to her, and she never brought up the subject again, even though I offered to help her find her birth parents.

When she was twenty, Bob called my husband to say that Sarah's birth mother wanted to meet her. She had written a lengthy journal for Sarah and also had photos and a gift for her. Bob gave us a photocopy of the journal for my husband and me to read, to decide if we wanted to give it to her. I gave the journal to Sarah on the same day that we received it.

About a week later, Bob arranged the meeting between Sarah and Christine, her birth mother. My husband did not agree with the meeting, but he wouldn't put a stop to it. Sarah caught me shedding a few tears on the day she was going to meet Christine; she immediately wanted to call off the meeting, but I insisted that she go. I knew that Christine was looking forward to it, and Sarah had already committed herself to going.

I asked Sarah, "How would you feel if Christine had changed her mind about giving you to us? You can't disappoint her now when you said that you would go."

She got ready and left with an armload of photo albums and her fiancé, Mark, for moral support.

Christine and her family came to Sarah's wedding ceremony, but the first time I actually met Christine face-to-face was two years after Sarah's wedding, at my husband's memorial service. I'd written her on a few occasions to express my gratitude, but it was good to meet her in person to say thank you and share a hug...and of course, a cry.

Matthew and Luke are polar opposites of Sarah, in that they have never expressed a desire to meet their birth parents. I am convinced that their close bond with their dad, Hans, influenced them. They just couldn't understand why Sarah would want to meet her birth mother. Two years after Hans passed away, I spoke to the boys separately and told them I would help them search for their birth parents; they both said no.

Christine's presence in Sarah's life continues to be a struggle for me. If I had my way, there would be no connection with Christine until I die—I realize that this is a selfish way to feel, though I wonder if an open adoption makes the connection easier.... Over the years, I've been thankful that our adoptions were not open. Christine can't be expected to understand how I feel because she hasn't walked in my shoes. And in the same way, it's impossible for me to fathom why she craves to have our families get to know one another.

One of my nephews, Tim, asked me after my husband's memorial, "What did you and Uncle Hans do to have your children turn out so well?"

At first I was a mouthful of teeth, but eventually I had a lot to say. A summary of my response was that, with God's help, we were willing to take on the challenge of being parents, even if that meant making some sacrifices. We knew that we were responsible to God, to each other, and to our children's birth parents, who had entrusted us with their children to raise them with love as our own.

Without a doubt, Sarah, Matthew, and Luke have been three precious gifts from God. Hans passed away on August 12, 2001, and the children have all struggled with the loss of their dad. They loved their father so much! But God is our strength. He never stops loving us. It continues to amaze me how God so faithfully teaches us more and more in our journey toward heaven. He has been with us every step of the way. All we have to do is trust his plan for our future in his perfect timing.

10

Pink Flowers

Christine, May 1999

In my relationship with God these days, we are mismatched in a difficult waltz. One step forward, six steps back. Occasionally I let God take the lead, then without warning I lunge away from him, spiral right out of his arms in an awkward jaunt straight into the nearest wall. No one's safe in my vicinity as I often knock over unsuspecting pedestrians—also known as my family—as I stumble. I read Hosea 11:2, "But the more I [God] called to him [Israel] the farther he moved from me" (NLT). *Yeah, oh yeah, that is so me.*

Anne frequents my thoughts. I hope she's doing better than I am. In the weeks following the reunion, she might have struggled emotionally, but I imagine she busies herself now preparing the million-and-a-half things required of the mother of the bride.

My hands aren't busy. I do the bare necessities for my kids, but I cling to the pages of my Bible and the simple stories of God working through other messy lives. The sisters, Mary and Martha, are a couple I figure Anne and I can relate to. Two vastly different women who don't see eye-to-eye, but who unite over the loss of their brother Lazarus. Anne and I, from a distance, struggle over the volatile reality of adoption reunion even as our hearts zero in on that one, shining, beautiful girl that we both named Sarah.

As the weeks lead up to Sarah's wedding, I obsess as I envision all the aunts, female cousins, and others invited to bridal showers, whereas I, the woman who gave birth to this bride, hear nothing. As I continue to twirl out of rhythm with the Lord, stepping on his feet and everyone else's, the gut-wrenching disappointment that Mary and Martha experienced with the Lord brings me strange comfort. That same weird solace I got from King David's life as he ran away from his son Absalom. It's not only that God took care of these people in their time of need that reassures me, but that I see my out-of-step dysfunction in these biblical lives.

For so long my faith convinced me that God was going to use my relinquishment of Sarah and our reunion for his purposes and blessings for all, and so on and so on. But now I worry my so-called quest from the Lord is again only a product of my overactive, wild, Technicolor imagination that ranks up there with any Hollywood producer.

I take comfort that the Lord's timing in the lives of Mary and Martha seemed to be as disastrous as it is in mine. If only he'd come to Lazarus's house when he was first summoned. If only God had done a better job preparing Sarah's family for the reunion. Or better still, if only he'd brought David into my life to marry me before I relinquished Sarah.

Still, the Lord consoled Mary and Martha separately, meeting them outside the village at different times. I envision Jesus waiting for them in a quiet shady spot, cooled from the hot sun under a large sycamore tree. Strong, practical Martha, weepy sensitive Mary. Strange how I see myself in both these sisters. Like me for sure, Martha used her knowledge of scripture as she tried to wheedle what she wanted from the Lord. At first she didn't want to accept her loss as part of God's grand scheme of things. She only focused on her personal loss kicking the insides out of her.

I have no idea what God wants to do with my relationship with Sarah and her parents, truthfully, being so unsure of his character at this point. But I can almost hear his voice, so tangible, reminding me that Anne and I are both his daughters, just as Sarah is....

A lovely thought, but it's not enough for me right now. I need more. Because here I find myself again—like I was during the search—running away like Hagar in the desert. Can I settle for this comfort alone—that God sees me, God hears my anguish?

Maybe I can settle for less than the warm relationship with Sarah that I crave. Not everyone on earth receives their dream come true. Can I be satisfied with emotional healing only? If I can be released from my emotional prison then perhaps I can console others. That might bring me some of the joy I lack. All around me people have their own hurts. Friends in adoption circles who are wounded for a variety of reasons, friends from church who suffer from illness, loneliness, or issues from childhood. I don't have far to look.

Rather sanctimoniously, with a tiny touch of noble martyrdom, I decide that with God's help I just might lighten someone else's load and stop striving to be Sarah's birth mom.

I've not been looking forward to Mother's Day this year. Just as she does every year, my Mum phones to wish me a happy day. But I trudge off to church in a defiant mood, trying to focus my thoughts as mother of only Lana, Kyle, and Robert, trying unsuccessfully not to think about Sarah as the five of us get out of our car and join the rest of our church family. Trying to put to death my unwanted maternal attitude for Sarah, I sing the choruses. A bit smugly, I sit back in the pew and enjoy the reading of a poem by one of the little girls, something about her mother's eyes. *See*, I remind myself, *being a mother is from the life shared together.* I am not Sarah's mother.

Then Krystal, one of the adopted girls in our church, crosses the platform to stand at the podium and starts to read a poem. She's not three lines into those stanzas when I start to weep. I work hard to put up the barriers, but in an instant the Lord wades into the breakers of my heartache. I try to push him away, but he holds me close with the words from an unknown author:

Legacy of an Adopted Child

Once there were two women
who never knew each other.
One you do not remember,
the other you call mother.
Two different lives
shaped to make yours one.
One became your guiding star,
the other became your sun.
The first gave you life
and the second taught you to live it.
The first gave you a need for love
and the second was there to give it.
One gave you a nationality,
the other gave you a name.
One gave you a seed of talent,
the other gave you an aim.
One gave you emotions,
the other calmed your fears.
One saw your first sweet smile,
the other dried your tears.

One gave you up—
it was all that she could do.
The other prayed for a child
and God led her straight to you.
And now you ask me
through your tears,
The age-old question
through the years:
Heredity or environment
which are you the product of?
Neither, my darling—neither,
just two different kinds of love.

As the reading of the poem ends, I soak up the pastor's topic on "It's not how we start out as mothers, but how we finish, that's important." And God whispers as if he's sitting in the pew beside me, "I never told you to stop being Sarah's birth mother."

Like we do most years on Mother's Day, David takes me and the kids out for lunch. After a meal of Chinese food, we arrive back at the house and the phone rings. At first I don't recognize the young woman's voice, and she repeats, "It's Sarah."

My hands tremble. Sarah? It is Sarah. *She's calling me, Lord. She's calling.* Her voice does sound like mine, as Bob said. For some reason I ask where Sarah is calling from. I'm hoping she's at home, with her mom right beside her, perhaps waiting for Sarah to pass the phone to her, and we can finally break down the wall of fear.

"I'm in my room. There's a houseful of company over to celebrate Mother's Day, so it's nice and quiet in here."

"You're in your room," I repeat inanely and try to imagine what that room looks like, how she and her mom must have decorated it. "We just got back from lunch out, Chinese food."

She laughs. "That's what we had too, only delivered."

Tamping down my excitement, my spiking joy, I ask her how university is going and drink in each tidbit of information as she chats about her finished semester and wedding plans. We talk so fast, like we did the day of the reunion, and I inwardly castigate myself when I hear how busy she's been. For forty-five minutes we talk, and she sounds so different. That protective barrier has been lowered today, and I hear in her voice a tiny bit of...dare I call it wistfulness? That image I had of her at our reunion as a bright student standing overly composed at a podium disappears, and over the phone comes the tentative voice of a young woman who doesn't have all the answers but fears she should.

"I was wondering," Sarah starts softly, and then it comes out a little stronger. "Will you be able to come to my wedding?"

I instantly swallow the miserable poison I've been swilling for weeks. "Yes, of course, we'd love to come to your wedding."

"Great!" The undiluted happiness in her voice feels like water to my drought-weary garden.

I want to stay in the present—somehow I know it's safer for her and me in the here and now—but my neediness to take us both back to the depths of our past is too strong. "Do you still have the little white Bible I sent along with a box of baby stuff, from when I relinquished you all those years ago?"

"Little white Bible?" She pauses. "Yes, I remember it, but it's been a long time since I've seen it...not sure where it is right now." I can almost see her glancing around her bedroom trying to locate where she last saw it.

"That's all right," I jump to reassure her. "No need to worry. I was just wondering if you ever saw those verses I underlined in the Psalms."

"You underlined some verses? For me?"

I give another half-laugh. "For you *and* your mom and dad. I can't remember the exact number of the Psalm right now, but it was something about seeing my children's children one day. I was kind of leaving a broad hint, at least what I thought was a broad hint, that I wanted to see you one day. And your parents."

"Oh, I don't remember if I ever noticed." She pauses again, and I picture her thinking back. "No, I don't remember," she affirms. "I'm so sorry. I wish I had noticed."

I laugh again, at myself, to put her at ease. So my ambiguous coded message of the underlined verses had done absolutely nothing. "That's all right. It doesn't matter. All that does matter is God brought us together now." *Oh dear Lord, was that too gushy?*

Then, when the conversation grows quiet—while twisting the coiled phone cord around my hand—and with the hesitancy of a beginner poker player, I ask, "So...do you think that you would like to work toward some sort of relationship? A...sort of birth mother/ birth daughter relationship?" A shiver runs through me that my stupid need to lay things out in the open may cause her to fly away like some exotic butterfly.

But her answer comes only a heartbeat later and in a small voice. "Yes...I think I do want to work toward that."

"Of course, I have no clue what that kind of relationship is supposed to look like." I attempt a confident laugh, so at odds with the high stakes I'm playing for.

She echoes that nervous laughter. "Oh yes...of course. I guess we just need to take it a step at a time."

My pent-up breath eases out, and I wonder if she's as exhausted as I am as we carefully hedge around the minefield of our future relationship.

With a return of that bravado, that bright student again at the podium, she adds, "I've always known that you loved me and that one day we would meet."

"I'm so glad," I murmur through a throat thick with the desire to cry. "You don't know how happy you've made me today."

A few minutes later as we hang up, my soul chimes with the knowledge that God confirmed my words to Sarah when she was just a tiny baby. Though she doesn't remember my ambiguous message in the little Bible, God preserved a seed of love in her heart for me.

I have to laugh. For the first time in months I laugh out loud with ridiculous joy.

Later that night I write in my journal, "Dear Lord, you did indeed encourage me to search for Sarah. You did send me that special long-stemmed pink carnation on the day of her eighteenth birthday that started the search."

Remembering back to February 23, 1997

A few weeks earlier David had caught me staring out the kitchen window. Sarah's eighteenth birthday was the next day, but I wasn't thinking of her that Sunday morning as I prepared for church, making sure I had all my Sunday school materials to teach my class of four-year-olds. I was more excited about the fun object lesson I'd devised for my little students. That week Lana had helped me cut out hundreds of colored construction paper fish. We'd tied string to bamboo rods to resemble fishing rods. In my bag of goodies, I'd stashed reams of crepe paper.

At church as our three kids hurried on to their own classes, David helped me overturn the two long tables my students normally sat at so that the table legs stuck upward. He went off to an adult class, and I proceeded to wrap crepe paper around the legs of each table so that with a strong dose of imagination it created the sides of a boat. Smiling to myself, I scattered the paper fish over the floor that would be a placid lake for the next hour just as the first of my students arrived. The four years olds were going to love this.

Most of the kids already stood in the makeshift fishing boats, holding their bamboo rods and trailing their string over the paper fish when Mary Pifer, the pastor's little girl, sallied in. Her mom waited by the door as Mary pranced into class in my direction. In her hand Mary held out a long-stemmed pink carnation.

"For me?" I asked

"Yes." Her mom smiled.

"What's the occasion?"

"Just because," Mary's mom said with a smile and a shrug.

Meanwhile, Mary had lost interest in the flower, grabbed a fishing pole of her own, and stood in one of the boats, pretending to be one of the Lord's disciples on a fishing trip.

Shivering with awe, I put the flower up to my nose to breathe in the delicate powdery fragrance. Sarah would turn eighteen tomorrow. How could it be that, practically on the day of her birth, the Lord had sent me this carnation, like those in that spring bouquet so long ago? Four-year-old Mary Pifer had no idea she was God's little messenger, nor did her mother. Could I dare believe this was his encouragement to search for Sarah?

But then, God never waited for his children to come looking for him. He pursued them instead. Like he searched for the one lost sheep while the other ninety-nine remained safe in the barn.

Searching for a biological family member was the scariest thing in the world. Already I trembled, just thinking that in one year's time Sarah would reach the age of majority, and we could legally meet.

I'd struggled so much as to who should search for who. Should I wait for her? But my motherly heart didn't want Sarah to feel one moment of the fear of rejection. I'd rather suffer that fear than have her feel it. I was the parent. I'd take the risk. God would give me the strength to emulate his Son. Wasn't that what being a Christian was all about?

Besides, the Lord had sent me these silly pink flowers for so many years. The time had come at last to find Sarah.

A South African Adoption—the Adoption of Susan
"My Dream of a Dark-haired Girl"
by adoptive mother Sheila Callanan

What a blessing to be brought up in a secure, though strict, home. I'd had a happy childhood with a loving earthly father who made it normal to see God as a loving heavenly Father. A father who taught me perseverance even when things got tough—he taught me through example. Sitting in church at the age of eight, being made to sing all the hymns and then listen to him preach after he had travelled miles in bad weather, only to find out when he got there that the only people in church were his family and the organist.

In my late teens I was also blessed to meet the man who would become my husband. We both wanted to start a family quite soon after marriage, and the thought of not being able to get pregnant never crossed our minds. Month after month nothing happened. This took me by surprise, and I went into panic mode. "God, what is happening here?"

Then the month came. I was late, ecstatic with the confirmation that I was pregnant, and I rushed to share the news.

In hindsight I wonder if this was a good thing. Although if the news is shared early and something happens, then those close to you can share the disappointment. Tears rolled down my cheeks as one day I sat in the bathroom with the evidence that there was not going to be a baby.

A woman's body has been preparing itself for a baby. Then it is gone and her body has to return to normal. The loss is real, and there has to be a time of grieving. Many don't understand this. Even my husband couldn't understand my tearfulness. He understands now.

How often I pleaded with the Lord to give us a child. I searched scripture hoping to find some verse that would confirm that one day I would have a child. The months went by—nothing.

Why were my friends and members of my family having babies? I didn't enjoy baby showers but attended them with a brave face although I ached inside. At church people tactlessly asked when we were going to start a family. My precious sister-in-law erupted into tears when she discovered she was pregnant for the third time—how was she ever going to tell me?

Three years had passed when God answered our prayers in a different way than what we thought. He impressed upon us that he was waiting to give us a child but that there were different ways that children could enter a home. Excitement began to sizzle.

We phoned the adoption agency for an appointment.

Six weeks before our appointment I had the most amazing dream, a dream where upon waking I knew that God was telling me something.

In the dream I had a little dark-haired girl. I called her Linda Joy. My husband told me he wanted to call her Linda Heather. The two names, we found out later, meant Beautiful Flower.

A week before our appointment I came down with a really nasty stomach bug. I could hardly lift my head off the pillow and couldn't keep down any food. I didn't want to cancel our appointment with the agency on the Friday morning, so the night before I went to the doctor to see if he could give me some medication.

Medication? I didn't need medication—the doctor's tests confirmed that I was at least seven weeks pregnant.

I felt so sick, the doctor's words didn't really sink in. Too late to cancel our appointment, we made our way to the adoption agency to tell them our news. From the moment of finding out about the pregnancy, I knew that we were going to have a dark-haired girl. We knew what we would name her. God had told us in my dream. Our beautiful flower.

Now I was confused though.

What was God trying to teach me when I had just come to the point of accepting that he had different ways of placing children in families? Maybe I still don't really know, but one thing I do know: God wanted this little dark-haired baby to be part of our family. On December 2, 1972 Linda Heather was born after a normal pregnancy with not even a hint of a miscarriage. I so enjoyed being pregnant—after the morning sickness had stopped, that is.

As for adopting a baby, I was convinced that the Lord had taken us on a journey of acceptance. I had my little girl, and God obviously in his wisdom did not want us to adopt, so what was the point of waiting? We would go straight ahead and have another baby.

We waited. Three years later we were still waiting.

Then I understood why God had let us walk that road before. We would once again apply to adopt a baby.

The only difference this time was that we felt we should go to a Christian agency. Back then in South Africa, an English family would not be allowed to adopt a baby from an Afrikaans mother. The adoption agency that we chose was predominately Afrikaans. It's not like that now, and adoptions take place across race and language, but because of this, back then, we knew we would have to wait longer for a baby. We phoned the adoption agency for an appointment.

11

The Giving

Christine, May 22, 1999

Today is another of those days I've dreamed of since I held each of my newborns. Cuddling them as babies, I'd pictured their milestones—learning to walk, hugging them goodbye that first day of kindergarten when I would leave them for only a few hours, their first overnight stay at summer camp, graduation, driving their first car, falling in love, and getting married. Most of those milestones I knew I'd miss in Sarah's life, but other than my extended hissy fit during those few months after the reunion, I'd always hoped, always prayed I'd see her wed. In spite of my brief departure from this desire, God has been faithful in fulfilling it.

I've heard nothing from Sarah or her family since that one phone call on Mother's Day. Though I checked the mailbox each day for an invitation to the reception, her wedding day is here at last. There's still no invitation, but I'm keeping my promise to Sarah.

David, Lana, Robert, and I arrive early at Sarah and Mark's church. Kyle's still too shy and remains at home. I want to be one of the first to enter, to see as much as I can, but most of all to find the spot where I want to sit, the place I've thought long and hard about. From the start David tries to cajole me to sit a little closer to the front, to the middle pews at least. After all, at this moment the church is practically empty.

There's a young woman setting up the table for the guestbook, and I sign my name, too shy to say who I am, not knowing if Sarah wants to make that public.

Slowly, guests arrive. Hymns from the organ and piano float across the sanctuary. At the first stanza of the Irish Hymn "Be Thou My Vision" my head lifts. *My favorite.* One of the myriad questions Sarah asked me the day of the reunion—"What's your favorite hymn?" Could she possibly have included this for me?

I study the guests as they arrive, trying to figure out who are aunts, uncles, and cousins. Like I would at any wedding, I play the guessing game of who resembles the bride...until it dawns on me. Of all the people in this church, the two young people beside me resemble Sarah most—tall, leggy Lana, and especially the little blond boy snuggled up to me, Robert. This is the wedding day of my firstborn, my birth daughter. White netting drapes from pew to pew, reminding me of the white lacy shawl that, in addition to the pink one, I wrapped her in when I sent her to her parents all those years ago.

Right next to where I sit, the central doors at the back of the church swing open. Mark stands at the threshold with the sweetest little grandmother. He sees me—*oh thank you, God.* Mark smiles at me, a special smile, and his "hi" comes out in a puff of excitement before he walks his grandmother down the aisle to her seat. *Thank you, Lord, for that treasure of a welcome. I see so much of you in him.* Then Mark escorts his mother down the aisle. So that's from whom he gets his smile.

At last the doors open and there is Sarah's mom. She's smiling a sweet smile too. Though Anne doesn't see me sitting at the very end of the pew right next to the door, not three feet away, for the first time I see her. This is my sister-in-Christ, this woman whom I've loved so long, prayed for, and wanted to know. My heart expands. God has answered both our prayers. It's such a happy and proud day for her, one in which she has every right to rejoice. It is *her* daughter's wedding day.

The relatives are all seated, and the doors open again.

My heart grows too big for my chest, and I hold my breath. There she stands. Just behind a line of flower girls and bridesmaids, on the arm of her father. So there is her beloved dad. Hans tucks Sarah's arm in his and tenderly lays his hand over hers. Music swells, and each attendant starts the slow wedding march, but I pay them little heed. Sarah is as beautiful as I've known she would be. I want so much to reach out and touch her.

I'm close enough to.

This is why I sat here, so that if she glances just a little to her left—God-willing—she catches my eye. If she sees that I am right here, so close. And if I am very, very courageous I just might step forward and hug her gently before she starts down the aisle. Dare I be so forward? That's what I've been imagining for weeks now, a miracle at this late date.

I lean out, half lift from my seat in the pew, praying, *Please let her see me.* But Sarah's gaze remains straight ahead. She glances neither to the left or the right, but way down the aisle to the young man who waits for her there, and that is as it should be.

I settle back again completely in my seat. It's not my place. And I shudder over what I've almost done, the gall I almost had, and it robs me of what little is left of my bravery.

The first notes of "Unchained Melody" pierce the air and hover.

My breath chokes me. That song! Oh God, how often did I hear that song and think of the day I'd see Sarah again? Sarah and her dad start down the aisle. Everyone rises while the music soars, and my loss of her along with joy creates a heady mixture in my blood. Weakness takes my knees, but I remain standing somehow. All is right. All is as it should be.

Their nuptials commence with the familiar description of love from 1 Corinthians 13. "Love is patient, love is kind. It does not envy...does not dishonor others, it is not self-seeking...not easily angered...keeps no record of wrongs...Love rejoices with the truth. It always protects, always trusts, always hopes, always perseveres."

Through my teary vision I catch Sarah's parents weeping too. As her dad gives her away from this point forward to belong to her husband, his actions echo mine from all those years ago. Only my goodbye to Sarah weighed in on a much sadder scale, and she will never cease to be Hans and Anne's daughter, like she ceased to be mine. Still, I think it's fair to say that today they might feel a tiny bit of my pain. Their little girl is gone. I gave Sarah to the Lord over twenty years ago, and today at her wedding I must give her back to God again, with the renewed understanding that she was never mine or anyone else's. *She's yours, dear God. She's yours.*

They're married and stride up the aisle together. As Sarah and Mark reach the back of the church, I'm standing right here, at the very end of the very last pew. She sees me at last...I think. Her face lights, but her gaze passes on. Perhaps it's someone else she's smiling at as the aisle fills with congratulating people. She's so happy. And that's what matters.

And then she passes by me and is gone.

As the aisle continues to fill with wedding guests following Sarah and Mark, David tugs at my arm, urging me to join the reception line. But I can't leave my pew. Hundreds of people mill around out there in the foyer, her family, her friends. A thousand conflicting emotions chain my feet to the floor. Fear mostly. Wanting so much, yet afraid to take the little that Sarah can offer at this time. I hang back, sit rigidly in my pew, twisting my hands in my lap, as afraid to venture out as I've been all these weeks not wanting to leave my house.

With sadness lining his face, his eyes bright with yearning, David begs. "Please, just come out to the foyer and say hello." But I can't move. He goes out himself with Lana and Robert and returns long minutes later. "Chris, if you don't hurry now, you'll miss your chance."

My chest is caught in a clamp. *Okay...okay.* I breathe. *Okay...go and say hello to your daughter on her wedding day. Stop being such a prickly fool!* I leave the sanctuary of my hidden pew and dash out to the foyer, but by the time I reach it, Sarah and Mark have already left. Their car is driving away, leaving the parking lot for their picture taking, and I curse myself. *You wretched, wretched fool.* Again, I've failed myself. I've also failed my kids. Lana silently seethes at me as we get into our car. Robert's confused, stares out the window. David understands but his frustration comes off him in soundless waves as he drives us home.

A few months later Sarah phones and tells me that she had made arrangements with the young girl at the guestbook table to give me a corsage. But I'd never said who I was when I signed the book. There had also been some cancellations for the reception, and Sarah had asked that someone at the wedding that day let me know so we could attend. But I'd not come forward. No one saw me. Too afraid to reach out for what God might have for me, I robbed myself of being there for all of Sarah's wedding.

I dwell on those love verses in 1 Corinthians 13 that were read that day. Most Christians know the words by heart almost as well as they know the Lord's Prayer. The problem with me is, as well as I know the words, I don't know how to live them. True love? I am rarely patient, not always kind. God forgive me, I do envy Sarah's parents. My lack of love kept me from rejoicing with the truth in the church foyer with Sarah and Mark. I've been running so long on a cup of love that is practically empty.

My mismatched waltz with the Lord continues. One step forward, three lunges back.

A South African Adoption—The Adoption of Susan
"If I Lay Eyes on This Baby, She's Mine"
by birth mother Vicki Blackwell

Attending high school at a Christian boarding school in Kenya—while my parents were missionaries in Malawi—was an amazing experience. At a school-wide revival I renewed my commitment to God and vowed to live totally for Christ. At the end of the term our family, stationed in Malawi, left for a stateside furlough. I began not only to slip away from my commitment, but to disobey deliberately.

Unaware that I was pregnant the next year when we left the States, I returned to the boarding school. As I gradually began to suspect, dread filled me. I knew, though, that I must face reality and so eventually trudged, heart pounding, down the hill from my dorm to the mission hospital on the same compound as my school.

There a pregnancy test confirmed what I already knew. Hospital staff conferred with school administration and told me that, under the circumstances, I couldn't continue my studies there.

Try as I might, I am unable to recall many of my emotions and even events of the next few months. When under stress, my memory suffers. Perhaps it is because subconsciously I blot unpleasant memories out. I know I called my parents and told them that I was being sent home. However, I cannot even recall the plane trip from Nairobi back to Malawi. I remember being afraid, anxious, and uncertain. I felt out of control and trapped by the circumstances.

There were days when I didn't want to live. My parents, though, were loving and supportive. The acceptance and encouragement of our mission families gave me hope and strength to carry on. I began the work needed to finish my high school education by correspondence.

I flew to Cape Town, South Africa to spend the last few months of my pregnancy in a maternity home operated by an Afrikaans-speaking Christian organization. Though it was frightening to go away alone, I knew that it was even harder on my parents. There were other girls pregnant and alone like me, and we were able to form friendships and support one another.

Any woman who has carried a child knows that the bond starts early and deepens as the little life within becomes more and more active. My parents and I had prayed about adoption. At seventeen, I could not support a baby nor offer the kind of life a child needed. My mind acknowledged that fact, but my heart did not. Until the last minute I argued with God.

At one point the doctors came in and pointed out to their interns that one could see and feel the baby clearly though it was before the day of ultrasounds. I could lie down for a nap, and if the baby was moving around a lot, I could rub its back and sing, and my little one would settle down.

Knowing what was best but hoping for something different, I prayed. I told God, "Lord, if I lay eyes on this baby, it's mine. If I don't, it's yours."

Labor began. I told the nurses, "I'm giving the baby up for adoption, so take it from the room immediately after delivery."

The labor was long, and as there was a shift change, that request did not get passed on to the nurses on the next shift.

I don't remember anything for twenty-four to forty-eight hours after the birth. I did learn I had borne a little girl. I asked what she looked like. Surprised, the nurse replied, "You sat up and looked at her."

Somehow learning that I had seen her but had no memory of it confirmed to me that I was right in letting her go.

I returned home to Malawi, finished high school, and prepared for college in the U.S. Busy but haunted with pain and depression over the loss of my child, I had dropped from a size ten to a size zero.

In college, though I had many good times, great sorrow and depression lingered. I cried a lot.

Counseling through my church helped, and my walk with the Lord again became a priority. I took my classes seriously. Still, years passed before seeing a pregnant woman or a baby no longer caused knots in my stomach and an ache in my heart.

I married Brent, a strong Christian man, and we had two precious daughters. My life was full in Louisiana. I still prayed for the child I had given up and dreamed of one day meeting her but was resolved that she was in God's hands.

12

ENGRAVED ON THE PALMS OF HIS HANDS

Christine, April 2000

An ancient cherry tree looms over the lawn outside MacMillan Hall, one of the student residences at Trinity Western University. Since last August, several months after Sarah's wedding, I've strolled past this tree on my way to the Mattson Center, where I began a new job as administrative assistant in the Financial Aid Department. Thanksgiving, Christmas, Sarah's birthday, and Easter, have all rolled past since the reunion, and now spring pulls out all the stops.

Soon Sarah will celebrate her first wedding anniversary, and I continue to thirst for that unique birth mother/birth daughter relationship. Why is it, after a full year, that Sarah and I just don't see each other much?

When we do, those short occasional visits are strained, like those two cartoon gophers Mac and Tosh working overtime in the politeness department. Except Sarah and I don't laugh much and seem only able to offer lackluster hugs upon greeting and tepid smiles as we visit. I'm sure it's because I don't know how to act that keeps her away. When she seems distant, I retreat, becoming equally as distant so that I stop myself for months at a time from phoning her. I'm paralyzed with the fear that I would only be bothering her if I did.

One day when Sarah, Lana, and I share a rare lunch date in historic Fort Langley, I wrestle with the fact that, though Sarah tells me about her day-to-day life and about her childhood, her protective barrier remains in place and as solid as the Berlin Wall. Yet, over coffee, her eyes light up and her smile goes warm when I tell her what Kyle and Robert are up to these days, and especially as she asks Lana about her life. She wants to know all about Lana's graduation, her mission trip last summer, and her plans for university. Deep down, I know Sarah really cares about her half siblings. Funny thing is, Lana is as shyly reticent as Sarah.

Other than polite and warm smiles, neither of my daughters show much emotion, but at least I know Lana. As for Sarah, I despair it's just toward me that she shows so little of her true self. My overblown neediness must be keeping her at arm's length. Later, when I ask David his opinion, he counters with, "Give the girl a break. May I remind you, Chris, you are not always the easiest person to read either? Besides," he adds, "Sarah strikes me as a very cautious person."

I know she's busy. For goodness sake, I keep reminding myself she's in university and her first year of marriage. Still, I want more of her to mend my fractured heart. It's not just losing my firstborn that's created this empty person that I am. All of my emotional bruising can't be laid at Sarah's doorstep. For the past year I've been counting up my losses. I blame my father for not filling my child-heart with love. I blame my parents' immigration to Canada that created such distance and few opportunities to visit my relatives in Ireland. And I blame life in general that David's relatives live an entire province away. I have recognized for years that I miss family, a sense of belonging to a greater web. It's hard for me to admit, but I think I'm lonely. How can I be lonely, though, when I have the best of husbands and three incredible children?

What's wrong with me?

My new job this past year helps, though. Trinity Western staff and students are great, but I hide my inner turmoil. At least I think I am.

But this April day on my way to work I stop to admire the cherry tree that has stood outside MacMillan Hall for generations. Blossoms cascaded in a veil of pink about a month ago, around Sarah's twenty-first birthday. Now only papery remnants swirl on the path, though a hint of pink lingers within the new leaves. And there, at the side of the trunk, a branch of straggling white blossoms toil upward as if gasping for notice. Part of the original graft? Or maybe just another tree stock stuck in the roots? But there it is, rebelliously protruding, something that should have been pruned away long ago. I stop for a moment and silently root for that wayward, pushy stalk. *Hang in there. No one may notice you, but I do.*

I am that straggling stock from Sarah's origins. How strange that this long-established tree with the unseemly shoot at its base should stand guard outside the very student residence that Bob Trainor and his family had lived in. This apartment complex, directly across the lawn from the building where I now work, is where he and Beverly had cared for baby Sarah those two days after I relinquished her in 1979. No doubt this massive cherry tree stood outside as their two little girls pushed my newborn infant in their baby buggy up and down the halls. Another miracle of pink flowers, Lord? What are you trying to tell me this time?

Whenever I tell people about the mysterious flowers that used to arrive each year—but now have strangely stopped—they wonder if those flowers were a miracle. A miracle? No, a miracle is when God heals a person. And I'm still bleeding emotionally over not having the relationship with Sarah that I crave. Even after a full year.

With this new job at Trinity, I don't cry as much, but I still fight it off. I've never spoken to a medical doctor, but I'm pretty sure I've gone through a severe bout of clinical depression, and I'm not sure yet if I stand on solid ground. I fear with my next step, or the step after that, I just might crash again into craziness.

At first I return to Bob for counselling, but after a while I feel he's too close to my personal story. I love how God used Bob in our lives. He and Beverly hold a special place in my heart, but I need a fresh set of eyes. Through connections in my church denomination I'm given the name of Dr. Garry Grams, a behavioral medicine specialist and family therapist in the Faculty of Medicine at the University of British Columbia. As much as I hate to admit it, I am not emotionally stable. As far back as that day I snuck into Sarah's high school, searching for her grad photo, I've recognized I am lacking something fundamental. Dr. Garry Grams has begun to counsel me, not so much by looking backward to past pain, but looking forward to what I want to be.

"You lost most of your childhood, Christine," Garry says during one of our early appointments. "You faced adult problems way too young, then barely into your adulthood you got pregnant and relinquished your baby, just when you should have been working on *you.* After that you didn't give yourself a chance—you got married and started a family. You never did the work on who you are. You're stuck in those emotions of an abandoned child, or of a young woman who's just given up her baby. That's why you keep on having these knee-jerk reactions."

My counselor's words align like solid bricks, something I can actually build with. I fill my lungs with a cleansing draught. If there's one thing I know how to do, it's how to work. If there's work I can actually do on myself—whatever that is—then by George I'll do it. Garry will guide me in that self-discovery over whatever number of sessions it takes.

In addition to Garry's suggestions, David has one of his own. He finds me crying, as usual, in the living room one day when I assume the house is empty. He goes out and returns a while later with a brand new journal and lapis blue fountain pen. Gently placing these items in my lap, he says, "Here honey, write it. You've been an artist all your life, either with paint or words. Write your book."

I've been journaling hit and miss over the years but penned reams during the relinquishment, and before and after the reunion. Like a blind man receiving his first braille writing slate and stylus, I accept my husband's gift. Is there something in this journey of mine that can help others? Journal after journal fills as I battle back and forth—should we have adoption reunions? Should we let the past remain buried?

A long time ago, I thought that Sarah, her mom, and I would be the poster girls for adoption. Well, maybe it's just me who's meant to be the poster girl for birth mothers. Should I rummage through the closet of my mind, drag out the old metaphoric placard for the rights of birth mothers? Should I march around bleating out my agenda—what I believe is the injustice of giving up one's child because you're poor in finances, lacking a husband, or just plain poor in spirit like I am? Even though I have so much and live in a wealthy country, I identify with that poor, pitiable woman in a third-world land. My heart aches for that deprived mother sitting in the dust, raising up a desperate face gaunt from hunger, flies assaulting her—because in this one thing we share—she too holds out her child for someone to save.

Dear God, who am I? That third-world woman? Hagar dashing out to the desert? Naomi who whines in her alter ego of bitter Mara? Hannah who also gave up her baby and has been blessed with more children? Digging for myself in God's Word isn't a bad place to start as I unearth parallels to my own life in those ancient and messy biblical lives.

Or is my true self to be found in what God wants? I always thought it rather autocratic the way he puts it in Romans 8:29: "For those God foreknew he also predestined to be conformed to the image of his Son, that he might be the firstborn among many brothers and sisters."

Oh yes, I know the words well. And I like the Lord Jesus Christ. That kind savior in the flowing white robe who doesn't shoo people away for blowing it. My liking for Christ has been growing year by year into an honest but lukewarm love. I really want to follow in his footsteps, be as loving as he is, but I'm scared by his brand of personal sacrifice. And God the Father? He wants to make me into a reflection of his Son, so the Bible says. If I attain that character quality, will the heavenly Father love me then, and stop playing favorites, putting better Christians before me? Christians like Anne and Hans, to whom he gave my child?

Then one day I read in Isaiah 49: "Can a mother forget the baby at her breast and have no compassion on the child she has borne? Though she may forget, I will not forget you! See, I have engraved you on the palms of my hands."

I stop and read it over and over again.

Engraved on the palms of his hands. Christ's painful atonement on the cross for the sins of mankind. And God compares his love to that of a mother. I understand maternal love, having known true sacrificial love from my mum. I saw it in myself at the time I relinquished Sarah, knowing then it truly was best for her to be raised by a mom and a dad.

Then I read again that interesting caveat as God says, "Though she may forget..."

This I understand!

I could never forget my kids. My love for Lana, Kyle, and Robert beats so strong at times I swear it will burst my heart. And I've been unable to cut my maternal ties for Sarah, though I tried for a short time. If I can't forget Sarah, but actually pine for her still, how much less can God forget me? My besotted love for my kids is often marred by my own neediness and grief, but it remains by human standards a powerful, primal devotion that will never cease. As a human being it is not possible for me to love others as described in 1 Corinthians 13. I know that now. Yet this very pulsing of my maternal heart is a smaller picture of God's great love. Though a pale thing compared to his love for us, it is the picture I understand.

"I will not forget you!" he says. His love is whole, perfect, unchanging over the eons, far more potent that the love of even better mothers than me, mothers like my mum, mothers like Sarah's mom.

As the understanding of his love seeps into me, another truth glimmers. It is a rare mother who doesn't experience failure on some level, some more than others. All mothers and fathers are wounded—so our love for our kids is flawed. When we grieve, we're not there for our kids. We fail them. Yet in my spirit I feel the Lord's soothing balm. *It's okay.* Christ died because I am imperfect. Instead of chastising myself, I need to fill up on God's leagues and leagues of love. The love verses in 1 Corinthians 13 that chastised me at Sarah's wedding now bless me instead.

Though I've been a Christian since a young girl and am now long past middle-aged, I count up the decades the Lord God graciously took to teach me this in easy-to-understand object lessons like those I give my four-year-old Sunday school students. He's been gently showing me through images I can grasp—pink flowers, songs on the radio, poems read at church, nature, other people's lives, especially those in his Word.

You love me. You are my Father. You are the daddy I've always wanted. I am as treasured as Sarah on her wedding day that her mother Anne had done so much to arrange. I am as equally treasured as when Hans took Sarah's arm in his and tenderly covered her hand before he walked her down the aisle. I am as treasured by God as my other three children are by David and myself.

Knowing the heavenly Father loves me as much as he loves Anne and Hans, as much as he loved King David, Mary, Martha, Hannah, Ruth, Naomi, as much as I've always known he loves my four children, my cup of love fills to the brim and overflows. I can forgive my dad for his neglect. Forgive Jim's parents for their inability to help me when I was pregnant with Sarah. And my anaemic pity for Anne and Hans's sadness over my reunion with Sarah transforms to actual love. I can afford it now. God has covered my so-called risk of rejection on the cross of Christ, and I see things in a different light. I can even forgive myself for my failures towards others throughout this journey.

Meeting Hans and Anne could never fill the void in me over the original relinquishment of my daughter. Even a relationship with Sarah could never make up for the loss of an earthly dad or the loss of my extended family through immigration in the early years of my life. And as much as I desire a close relationship with all of my children—including Sarah—I am designed for a close relationship with my heavenly Father.

With this fresh, sparkling love fizzing through my veins, I lighten up on Anne and Hans. I have no right to be upset with them, and they have every right to keep their family life private. In Anne's letter she talked about God's timing surrounding the adoption of her children. Deep in my bones I always knew I was too emotionally unstable to be integrated into their family at the time of my reunion with Sarah.

Now each day when I pray for Sarah and Mark, along with the rest of my kids, I'm thankful for whatever spot Sarah can offer me in her life. I no longer need to become an extension of the VandenBos family. But I pray, *Someday, Lord...someday, bring Sarah and me closer, just a little closer, please.*

From Cape Town South Africa—Susan's Adoption
"Carry Mommies and Weddings"
By adoptive mother Sheila Callanan

In many respects I am placid by nature and handle crisis pretty well. Not so on March 22, 1978 when the telephone rang and the voice on the other end of the line said, "Am I speaking to Mrs. Callanan?"

When I answered her in the affirmative she went on. "Did you and your husband apply for adoption?"

My heart thumped. "Yes."

"Well I am phoning from the adoption society to let you know that we have a little girl for you."

Then I did the craziest thing—I asked her to hold the line for a moment and ran across the road to my "bestest" neighbor and shouted through her window, "The agency is on the phone and they have a little girl for us." Poor social worker, she must have wondered where I'd got to. Still with my heart pounding, I sprinted back to speak with her, breathless.

"Mrs. Callanan," she said, "there is a slight problem."

Babies with any medical problems or deformities were never placed in homes for permanent adoption. The baby they considered for us had been born with a club foot and would need a lot of medical care in the next few years. However, after praying, the agency hoped to give her to us, believing this baby was meant for our home.

Without hesitation I assured her we wouldn't mind at all, but she insisted I call my husband first, just to make sure Edwin was also okay with this.

Two and a half years ago we had applied and waited for this phone call. As I shared this with our matter-of-fact little Linda, she turned to me and said, "Let's call her Susan."

The next afternoon in the reception room, with racing hearts we stared at the door, willing it to open and bring us our new baby. At last a member from the agency placed the tiniest little girl all wrapped up in a pink blanket into my arms. At two weeks old, she weighed only six pounds.

As I gazed down at her I could not take it in. *This is our child.* A child given to us because a group of people had prayed they would be guided to choose the right family. A child had been given to us because a girl had made a difficult choice.

Deep down in my soul I wept for that girl. Who was she, what were the circumstances? I would honor that choice and do everything in my power, through the grace of God, to give her child a stable, happy, and secure upbringing.

A plaster of Paris encased little Susan from her toes to her thigh for the first thirteen months of her life. Her leg was in a frog shape. In the year to come, my paranoia over keeping the plaster clean meant I continually cleaned it with shoe whitening. I changed her diapers in an instant, wanting nothing to run down into the cast. Throughout some painful medical procedures, this sweet, friendly little girl hardly ever cried.

From an early age, Edwin and I, through storytelling, introduced Susie to the fact that she had a "Carry Mommy." When she was older we assured her that if she ever wanted to find her birth mother, we would support her in her search. We received no counseling on how to tell a child they were adopted. We never read any books. God gave us the wisdom because he was already working out his plan.

"Before I formed you in the womb I knew you, and before you were born I consecrated you" (Jeremiah 1:5 NASB).

This is the story we told Susie from the time she could understand.

> Once upon a time there was a daddy and a mommy.
>
> They were very happy because God had given them a daughter, but they were also sad because they so wanted to have another little baby in their home and a brother or sister for their daughter. No more babies could grow in the mommy's tummy.
>
> And then they heard of a mommy who had a baby she loved very much but who couldn't look after it and give it the things that babies needed, so she prayed to God and asked him to find a new mommy and daddy who would be able to care for the baby.
>
> So one very exciting day the new mommy and

> daddy went to fetch the baby and took with them clothes, a bottle, a pink blanket, and one bootie.
>
> Do you want to know why there was only one bootee? Because the baby's leg was in plaster of Paris. The daddy, the mommy, and the big sister were so excited and loved the little baby.

One day when we knew she was ready, we changed the mommy and daddy to our names and the baby's name to hers.

Delight flooded her little face. And so she learned about being adopted.

Being adopted—not something we spoke about every day as most of the time we didn't even think about it—became a normal, natural word in our home. We had a funny little incident once. After a naughty episode, Edwin prepared to mete out some discipline to Susie when she informed him that he couldn't discipline her because he wasn't her father!

"Oh yes I can," he said. "Come with me to my cupboard and I will show you a piece of paper that says you are my child."

As mentioned previously, we had told her that if she ever wanted to find her "Carry Mommy" we would help her. Only once in all her childhood did she ever make mention of finding her, and it came out unexpectedly. She was about eight at the time, and when riding home from school she suddenly asked, "Are we doing anything today?"

"Not really."

"Well then, can we go and find my Carry Mommy?"

That wasn't, however, when her search began.

At quite a young age Susie met her future husband, JeanRay. They dated for some four or five years before they got married when she was twenty. Around this time she developed a strong desire to find her mother. In her heart she wanted to let her mother know she was happy, doing well, and getting married. After her soon-to-be husband completed his studies, they were preparing to enter the ministry.

Together, Edwin and I had made a promise to Susie. It was time to keep our word and walk that road with her. Utter peace enveloped my soul. I was ready and excited to see how this was going to pan out. Not even a slight pinch of anxiety or jealousy disturbed me because I knew that even if she found her mother and they developed a relationship, it could never be the same as the relationship we shared. I wanted Susie to own her history and to do with it whatever she wished. I trusted God to control any negative feelings because I believed he was ready to do a miracle.

And so we made an appointment to see the social worker at the agency. As Susie was still under twenty-one, I was required to go with her and give my permission for the agency to draw the file. The social worker opened a brown folder and started reading....

In awe Susan and I listened to the social worker read the facts regarding her biological family background.

While there were many things we did not know, we did know Susan's birth surname. When we went to sign the one adoption document at the magistrate's office all those years ago, her birth mother had been before us to sign that same document. In addition, we had been told that her biological grandparents were missionaries, but we'd assumed they were missionaries in South Africa when in fact they served as missionaries in another African country. How interesting to discover we belonged to the same church denomination.

Uncanny similarities mounted. The agency had been so sure we were the right family for Susan that they looked past the physically dissimilarities. Susan, being fair and petite, didn't look like us at all.

Time to take the next step. Where does one start? After much consideration Susan decided she would delay the process until after the wedding. With so many emotions around getting married, she didn't think she could cope with the emotions of trying to find her mother. We had been told that statistically there would only be a twenty percent chance that things would work out well. Susan had to be prepared for this, confident in her identity in Christ, not in whether she found her mother or not, or whether she would be accepted or rejected.

Six months later an eager Susan wanted to start the process again, but hesitated, wondering whether Edwin and I were really ready for her to start the journey. We had told her that we were, but did we really feel ready? God confirmed in her what we had always told her when I brought up the subject myself and asked when she was going to call the agency again.

We went back to speak to the social worker. This time, her husband came with us.

The social worker created a plan entailing our attempt to contact the grandparents through the American Embassy in the country where they served. We knew that this would take a while. This process is not for the impatient.

Our first experience of God's miracle and seeming coincidences occurred just after we had been to the adoption agency. That Eastertime Susan asked me to accompany her to an all-day church function. I only had one hour free, but in our brief time at the church we met a missionary couple serving in the same country as Susan's biological grandparents. Naturally I asked this couple if they knew them. Amazingly, they never asked why we wanted to know or to explain our connection with their friends.

Imagine the feelings and emotions that passed over us when they said that they knew them well, and that if I phoned the next morning they would provide me with a phone number and e-mail address. Wow, God! Instead of waiting weeks and weeks we only waited a few days.

Now we held details in our hands. Should we make a phone call or write an e-mail? Would it be right for me to make a phone call and say something? "Oh hi, my name is Sheila and I adopted your granddaughter." How would her grandparents react if they didn't even know that they had a granddaughter? Even though we were so excited to speak to them, wisdom prevailed, and we phoned the agency and gave them the details.

13

Reflection in a Dark Mirror

Christine, 2000

With David's constant encouragement, I keep on writing. Though genuine love grows within me for Sarah and her family, I still struggle with the issues of adoption as a whole. I still wonder if I should have ever given her up in the first place. Eventually I finish the first draft of my non-fiction birth mother book and give it to my counselor. When I return to Garry's office a few weeks later, I find him at his desk, leaning back in his chair, his fingers steepled and a smile of quiet dignity on his face. "Author, author. I want to be the first to say that to you."

"Really?" I gush, grinning like a fool. "You honestly think so?"

"Yeah, I do. Your writing is an aspect of the real Christine. People need to grieve their losses, but I think this is where you should focus now, develop this gift from your heavenly Father."

"The real you," my counselor says. I hardly know myself. *Hmph!* The adult me that I'm most familiar with is an intense person with an overly sensitive knee-jerk reaction to emotional pain. But I find hope when I read past the love description in 1 Corinthians 13.

"When I was a child, I talked like a child...reasoned like a child. When I became a man [woman], I put the ways of childhood behind me. For now we see only a reflection as in a mirror; then we shall see face to face."

The Lord uses our lives to teach us how to be like his Son, but the pixels of another thought multiply and take shape. When I first saw Sarah's grad photo that day in her high school, I had hoped for a reflection of me. When it comes to my other three children, it doesn't matter if they look more like David than me. But I'd hoped—imagined—all these years that Sarah and I would share a strong physical resemblance. Whenever I envisioned her as a child, it was a skinny blond ghost that I saw growing up in that wonderful childhood. During the search for Sarah, I'd been looking for my phantom child to be sure, but it became clear that I was also searching for that phantom me.

But who is that person? A reflection of my relinquished daughter? Or a reflection of God's Son? After all, that's what the Lord wants.

Both seem such extremes—one the image of what I've lost, and the other something fit for heaven that might bless others here on earth. Deep down I want to be the latter. Sarah is herself, and I want to be me. But as I study the powerful chapter eight of Romans, I ask—do we have to know who we are *first* in order to *then* let Christ make us into a likeness of himself? Or is it possible that my true reflection, which seems to be imprisoned in a dark mirror, is to be released and made clear as I gradually grow into the image of God's Son?

Garry, from the Faculty of Medicine at UBC and also a devout Christian, affirms my thinking. Romans 8:28 says that "in all things God works for the good of those who love him, who have been called according to his purpose." All along, God has been using the heartache that life sent me to redirect my losses and grief into an ever-increasing goodness as I obey his Son's commands. Only God can use my heartbreak to form the clay of me, cut away the rubbishy bits, fire it in the kiln, and then polish the daughter he's always known I would become. A large part of me is a writer, a communicator, one who wants to share with others my bumpy journey to God.

And so I figure that must mean God wants me to write a birth mother book that portrays their losses and rights. I should try to get it published.

For a year I work to garner interest in that book, but no doors to the publishing world open. Not even a sliver. Whenever I share with people about my writing, quite often they give me a perplexed smile, and a patronizing tone laces their words. "Good that you have a hobby. Must be so cathartic."

Thank God I have friends who don't think I've just arrived from Mars. My writing is not a hobby but something seeded in me as far back as the days when I sat in the maternity ward and held baby Sarah. Or farther back to when I was a little child sitting on the kitchen floor at my blackboard, drawing and telling myself stories. And I'm sure by this time that all the catharsis I needed from writing is complete. I've been on the Lord's pottery wheel long enough. Surely my time in the kiln is over. I'm ready to launch what my experience has taught me about the Lord on the world. *Just let me at 'em.*

Typical. Most people going through emotional healing think they're healed long before they actually are.

My journey to publication is like my search for Sarah—agonizingly slow. But I am learning, and I control my urge to growl at the Lord and pray with only a hint of my old whine, "Okay, okay, if you don't want me to write this non-fiction account, how *do* you want me to use this writing gift?" The impression gradually emerges that I'm to paint what I've gained of emotional and spiritual healing into fiction to—God-willing—help others. *Ha, that's a laugh.* I'm far from the mature Christian I want to be, but I see the seasoned vintage of Christian beauty on a daily basis in the staff and faculty I work with at the university. At least I have the sense to watch and learn from their example.

What's more, the Trinity staff members are given the benefit of one free academic course per semester. Over my nine years working here, I sign up for every course on Creative Writing and Journalism they offer, as well as a few courses in Fine Arts. Professors like Lynn Szabo and Loranne Brown feed my starving creative mind. My kids get a kick out of my desire for study. Like the time Kyle recognized my love for Sarah only affirmed my love for him, the kids blossom in the understanding that a healthy mom is one who enjoys learning and growing. My work on myself like Garry said—to become the woman God wants me to be—is a good building block to a healthy family. Lana, who's become a student at Trinity, has even taken an art course with me.

Like a Polaroid photo gradually deepens in color, as shapes coalesce, the artist in me surfaces—the artist I never gave a chance to develop when I entered young adulthood so long ago. Now my face goes warm in the pride my children and husband have for me.

Bit by bit, I work on a fictional manuscript until it's finished. The publishing doors begin to squeak open. One day a guest comes to Trinity to offer a seminar on literary representation. David Sanford, a published author and expert in communications, is looking for writers. We strike up a conversation over the coffee urn, and I share my birth mother story while David Sanford smiles and shares that he and his wife are the proud parents of an adopted daughter, Anna. Shortly after that meeting David signs me as a client, and he becomes my first literary agent.

David and his wife, Renée, contact me as they are compiling a book about adoption. In October 2008, in partnership with Focus on the Family, they publish *Handbook on Thriving as an Adoptive Family*. When my love letter to adoptive parents is included in the Sanford's book, I'm satisfied. It isn't my full story, but maybe it isn't God's plan for that fuller story to be published. I think maybe this fulfills my vision from all those years ago, that my birth mom experience will encourage others.

And I'm happy. My marriage is strong and growing happier each year. Lana is in her last year of university. Kyle is a young adult and busy with his own life too. Rob, our youngest, is growing into a fine musician. And in 2009 my unpublished novel wins the American Christian Fiction Writers' Genesis Award. *Shadowed in Silk* is a novel, I might add, that has absolutely nothing to do with adoption but is a romantic historical based on my Hagar in the desert theme—that no matter how invisible we feel we are to others, God sees us, hears us, and cares.

Now all I have to do is find a publisher.

Throughout the writing of that novel, a relationship between Sarah and me grows about as quickly as a coral reef. Less than an inch per year. I still hardly know her. One of her strengths is that she's a terrific listener. No wonder God directed her to become a nurse. In Sarah's presence I find it too easy to unload my own problems, my confusions, even some minor medical ailments, because she exudes compassion.

On one of our rare occasions, David and I make the trip down to Washington State to visit Mark and Sarah. As the two men chat easily, Sarah sits on her couch and curls her legs up under her. I join her in their trendy vintage living room filled with photos and art from their travels around the world, many of which are medical mission trips. One of Sarah's three kitties saunters in, and she reaches down and lifts it up to her lap, giving the cat the petting it so vocally insists upon. With her smooth dark blond hair tied back in a messy bun, Sarah tilts her head and focuses her blue-gray gaze on me. Usually, depending on the topic of conversation, her face will soften with a slight smile or crease with a gentle frown. Yet behind that steady gaze a brilliant mind works on how to alleviate the other person's pain—in this case, mine.

Today, at Sarah's encouragement, I tell her the plot line of my novel. Her brows rise higher and higher, her petting of the cat grows more energetically distracted as she listens intently to my every word. "I can't wait to read it," she says. "Wow, that's so cool that your ancestors were soldiers in the British Raj."

I smile and remind her that they are her ancestors too.

"Oh, right." She grins, a little abashed.

As David and I drive home from their place though, I hope that my interpretation is correct. I hope she was only pleasantly disconcerted that she shares my biological ancestors. But I worry that my reminder of her connection to my bloodline is only an annoyance, that she prefers to remember only her place on her adoptive family tree. Then I remind myself, it's natural to inspect every detail, every word when a relationship is in trouble. But maybe it was time I started to let this old habit go. Maybe a warm relationship between Sarah and me was actually starting to grow.

Still, on the drive north to the Canadian border, questions clatter in my mind—why does Sarah tell me so little about her own inner struggles? Or is she such a good listener that it doesn't occur to her to speak about her own feelings? Her dad passed away quite a while ago, and no doubt that takes a long time to grieve. Is Sarah still protecting her mother's feelings over our relationship?

After ten years, the fact that we still don't know each other well has to be because I do all the talking. Strangely, I also know that if I made more of an effort to drive down to Washington State and clammed up on what I was feeling, I'd probably see more of the real Sarah. My birth daughter isn't the only one putting up protective barriers all these years after our reunion. Mine is a wall of words.

But during these past ten years of Mark and Sarah's marriage, she has shared with David and me briefly that she's lost a number of babies to miscarriage. Three that I know of for sure, but I suspect the number is higher.

This kind of immense loss on top of losing her beloved dad strikes me dumb in a hallowed sort of way. Like Isaiah, I am silenced to quiet shock—not at seeing a vision of God, but at seeing Sarah's pain. A pain that in my mind is as costly and bitter as myrrh, one of the oils used to anoint the crucified Christ. I want to be one of those who bring comfort and hope to her, but I recognize that the emotional braces in her life are her immediate family, her husband, her mother and brothers, her in-laws. From a distance I can only add her heartache to my daily prayers, that God will allow her to have a miracle baby.

And at least with my obsessive, zealous personality focused on becoming a writer, I'm giving the poor girl peace to get on with her life. Though the pendulum of my faith hasn't yet learned to stop swinging quite so far in extremes, I recognize that I am changing. I'm certainly not the person I was five or ten years prior.

So now, why do this morning's devotions, the deep and thoughtful words of Oswald Chambers from *My Upmost for His Highest*, tap me on the shoulder? "...the Spirit of God will show us what further there is to be relinquished... There will always be a painful disillusionment to go through before we do relinquish."

Oh dear Father, I've been through a number of painful disillusionments. As we all have. Before and after the reunion, I thought I'd fully viewed myself for what I was and corrected the trajectory of my life. Haven't I learned one of the greatest lessons of my life through the painful loss of my firstborn—the depths of God's love? At least I'll never have to relinquish another of my children to gain spiritual wisdom. *But dear Lord, what valley of sorrow do you want me to go through next?*

Because Sarah isn't the only daughter I hardly know.

I've been working at Trinity Western for some years, with Lana attending as a student. For the past few years she's lived in dorm, but even before she moved out of the house, I should have seen the signs.

It's almost time to go home as I file work away at my desk in the Registrar's Office, when Lana's dorm leader and a staff member from Student Life approach my desk. They ask to speak to me privately, their expressions heavy. I know that look. *Oh dear God, I know that look.* I've seen it plenty of times when other parents of university students are told something awful has happened to their child.

I go as still as stone, only shaking my head. "No. No, just tell me. Whatever it is, just please tell me...now."

My fear stretches across the expanse of my desk toward the woman from Student Life as she says, "Lana is in the hospital. She took an overdose of pills last night."

A South African Adoption—the Adoption of Susan
"Early Morning Phone Calls"
by birth mother Vicki Blackwell

My parents had moved to the Southern African country of Lesotho. Brent and I saved enough money for plane tickets and flew the nine thousand miles between Houston and Lesotho with our five-year-old and eighteen-month-old daughters for a three-week visit with them. It was a memorable time with grandkids getting to be with their grandparents. I had no idea at the time how I would come to cherish that visit.

After returning home to Louisiana, I received an early morning call from my dad. "Your mom...she's gone!" A car accident had suddenly taken her life.

Again great sorrow filled my life. Dad came home to Louisiana, and we buried my mom. He returned to Lesotho alone but shortly afterward came back to the States for a furlough. God had a plan for him. The first person I called about Mom's death after immediate family had been Rebecca, who, along with her husband, had served with my folks in Malawi. Her husband had died years earlier of leukemia. I had always called her Aunt Rebecca, as is the custom with missionary kids.

Dad married Rebecca, and they returned to Lesotho, the mountain kingdom, with horse saddles and other equipment to ride into the mountains to share the gospel. Lesotho was a difficult and somewhat dangerous place. I remembered the high security fences, the dogs, the barred windows, and the night watchmen at all the houses in town. Political unrest kept everyone on edge. Frequent skirmishes between the police and army meant gunshots and cannon bursts even in residential neighborhoods.

Once more our phone rang early one morning. With dread I insisted that Brent answer. Was it more bad news?

"It's your dad," he said. "He sounds excited."

As I took the phone, Dad said, "We got a call from an adoption agency."

My first thought was, they're going to adopt a child! Then I realized he was talking about *my* adoption.

"Her name is Susan," he said. "She is married to a young man studying for the ministry..." He went on to tell something of her past and her plans for the future.

Susan wanted to make a connection!

Susan and I exchanged e-mails and pictures. In her first picture she was wearing an Indian sari—she had been on a mission trip to India—and she looked so much like my mother!

As God would have it, my new sister Melanie, Rebecca's daughter and my dear friend, was planning a trip to visit our folks. We booked flights together and arranged to meet them and Susan's family in Cape Town.

The trip from Houston to Cape Town was a long one. I had worked at my hospital job right up until time to leave and knew that I had only a week to spend in Cape Town. Never able to sleep on a plane anyway and so keyed up, I certainly got no rest on this flight. I think I talked Melanie's arm off. The more exhausted I became, the more I worried I would be too lethargic to interact well with Susan and her family.

I needn't have worried.

14

The Reaping

Christine, March 2006

Boys don't always notice when Mom isn't all she should be. Daughters are different, as though they're looking to their mothers as a rough sketch of what it will mean for them to be women, rejecting and incorporating aspects of us as they grow.

In the early years when the kids were little, before I started the search for Sarah, I can honestly admit that I filled their early childhood with home-baked cookies, family vacations at summer camps, bright Christmases. I cared for their smallest needs, tucked them in at night with a kiss and a hug. With each child at their various individual tuck-in times, I told them about the Lord Jesus. At different times in each child's life, safe and sound in their beds, I led them one-by-one to faith in Christ. I was a good mom...then.

During the search and reunion, the boys were too young to notice my struggles for stability, especially since they had a great dad who made up for it all. In the years after the reunion, with good therapy and a renewed focus on God's Word, I returned to the mom I used to be, even striving to be better.

That shining day from a few years ago—when David and I took

Lana out to lunch after church and I told her about Sarah for the first time—continues to glimmer in my memory like a favorite Christmas ornament. For the first time, my daughter saw the real me. But I want Lana to see not just the mom I used to be, but the person in whom the Lord Jesus is reflected. I want Lana and my boys to see that God, in that scintillating way of his, continues to work on the genetic code he's written into our beings when we were but babes in the womb and uses our lives to perfect and polish us until we shine.

But off and on during those two or three years of Lana's impressionable teens, I'd let depression, poor self-esteem, and my own suicidal thoughts filter in to my children's lives. Lana took emotional refuge at her friends' houses, friends who often only added to her confusion. No matter how much I've changed since then, the damage was done.

For the first time I'm seeing that my precious Lana, my girl, is also one who doesn't openly share the deep things of her heart. Neither one of my daughters blurt out their feelings like I do or wear their emotions on their sleeve. Like Sarah, Lana listens carefully when others confide their joys or hurts, giving little away of her own turmoil. And if you're not paying very, very careful attention you'll never know that Lana is going through canyons of pain. I didn't.

The only consolation I have is that I'm not entirely to blame. That susceptibility for emotional fragility is also a genetic baton handed down to me and my offspring from previous generations; grandparents, my own mother, an uncle. Perhaps my father's alcoholism is an indication of that kind of emotional frailty.

As I break the speed limit on the way to the hospital, that consolation is so small, a Band-Aid on an open wound. Once again I'm battling the fear that plagued me after the reunion. Have my failures as a fractured mother—those blasted two or three years when

I closed myself away crying, those times I'd gone off on long drives alone, thinking thoughts of running away or killing myself—caused my child to do something so heartrending?

The thought that my beautiful girl is so unhappy she tried to take her life is entirely different from the pain of losing Sarah. This isn't the pain of cold gray elevator doors closing between me and my child. The pain of knowing how much Lana is hurting sears my heart and soul. If I lose Lana, then life will be as dark and futile as ash, an anguish I cannot bear.

As I enter the emergency ward I catch a glimpse of her by the far wall. My tall, willowy daughter in a hospital bed, propped back against pillows, covered by a warm blanket. All other sights and sounds fall away to a dark tunnel around me. My child sits in an overly bright alcove, under white sheets, a pale peach hospital gown sagging from her neck and exposing her delicate collarbone.

She looks up and starts to cry as I near her bed. Even from a few feet away I see her tremble. Something deep inside me dies. I *have* done this to my child. She lifts a hand to wipe her cheek like the little girl she once was, as vulnerable as when I used to hold her hand to cross the road. Vulnerable but alive! It could so easily have been otherwise, but God protected her. We both still breathe, our hearts still pump. Though we're both bruised as crushed reeds, there is hope. I'll give my all to see her find joy.

Sitting down beside her bed, squeezing her hand, I weep as I tell her, "I love you. More than life itself."

She nods, tears streaking her pale and tired face, and whispers, "I know, Mom. I know you love me. I kept telling the nurses all day to phone you...."

Lana's despair has been going on for a long time, but I failed to notice her slipping further and further into the black hole of depression. She hid her unhappiness so well. She's always been a quiet person, more a listener than a talker. I thought it was just Lana's way when she offered only polite smiles as she talked of generalities, her classes, or a recent essay. I thought she was happy. Now I know that distant but serene façade covered up a raging river of pain.

With her lying in a hospital bed, the scars of her emotional pain so terribly visible, nothing is hidden. She holds her head low, like a bent flower stem, so that her long sleek hair falls forward, veiling much of her face. There's no light in her eyes, only deep mirrors of sadness. At least by letting me see her cry, she's inviting me into her life again. But then I remember, Lana was always shy about saying how she felt, even as a tiny girl. David and I thought she was just well behaved. Her dad and I are learning for the first time that Lana can't see how beautiful or smart she is. She thinks she's worthless.

Is it possible that I gave that impression to my treasure of a daughter?

Lana assures me I hadn't, and I have the common sense not to blame myself for all of her depression. Still, though God has worked enough on my person these past few years, I have to admit I am responsible for much of her sorrow. I sowed the seeds when the soil was most receptive.

It wasn't my search for Sarah that hurt Lana, she assures me. It's not my longing to have Sarah as part of our family. She loves Sarah and wants her in our family too. Thinks of her as her sister. But I know what hurt Lana, though she cannot say it to my face. It's not about Sarah at all. The little Lana can tell me of my contribution to her depression will take months and years in the telling. But my old crazy times have done this, those times when my practically empty cup of love caused me to act out. As I sit in the hospital holding her hand, I accept that I am reaping the harvest of pain that I planted.

But God is the God of resurrections, the God of new beginnings. This time I choose to believe. I choose to relinquish my Lana to God the Father, so that he can sow renewed joy into her being. *Our family needs a new garden, Lord, a garden of joy.*

A few months after Lana is released from hospital, she shares with me a strange nightmare she once had. In her dream she looked into her mirror and instead of seeing herself, she saw the reflection of a face like Michael Jackson, a poor soul who'd messed and messed with the face God had given him. Lana thinks she's ugly, something too broken for anyone to ever want. In my bedroom across the hall from hers, I feel her loneliness and know she cries, wondering if there will ever be someone special for her. All she wants is what most women want—to be loved by a special man, to one day have children.

There's no way to go back and fix the past. Only forward. Lana needs to learn the same painful lesson I learned—that who we are is to be found in Christ.

Too many of us feel like rough sketches of ourselves. Too many blank spaces, eraser marks from where we tried to improve on our own and failed. The rough sketches of us contain coarse pencil lines rendering what isn't there and entirely missing what is. We need to do what the artists of old did when they learned their craft. They studied the work of master artists and copied their perfection until they developed their own skill. We need to look into the finished portrait of Christ's face to find our own.

I pray for each of my kids every day, but these days after I pray for my sons, I pray extra hard for my daughters. Both are going through so much pain, that bitter holy myrrh that anointed the broken body of Christ. I know my daughters' heartaches too well—Lana in her inability to see how beautiful, how special she is, and Sarah losing the babies in her womb. How strange that through these miscarriages Sarah is feeling the loss of an empty womb similar to mine as her birth mom when I couldn't keep her, and that of her mother Anne who suffered the emptiness of infertility.

Sarah's sadness is clear in a Facebook message on Mother's Day one year. "This has not always been an easy day for me nor many, many others. For those who have lost their mom or their child, struggled with infertility, or relinquished their child for adoption—please know you are thought of and loved."

As I groan in my spirit along with my daughters, the words of Oswald Chambers in *His Utmost for His Highest* bring some strange comfort. "The first thing God does with us is to get us based on rugged reality... Why shouldn't we go through heartbreaks? If through a broken heart God can bring his purposes to pass in the world, then thank him for breaking yours."

Does God allow our hearts to be broken on purpose?

If so, how can I possibly be thankful for the pain I've gone through in my own life and now see in my daughters? Even knowing "you are not your own" (1 Corinthians 6:19), that we belong to God, can I believe that God broke the hearts of my two daughters and mine on purpose? Is God really that cruel? Is he letting us all down? Forgetting about us?

No, no, a thousand times no! I want to shout. Through my bumpy road I've seen that he is not cruel. He never forgets us.

But when I search out answers to this question, I find that even Christian theologians have no definitive answer. Many of us waver back and forth. "Yes...maybe God does allow us to suffer on purpose." Then we shift to the other foot. "But then again, he is not the author of the world's suffering. So no...I'm not sure.... There are scriptures for both points of view."

As I read further with other theologians, I'm reminded that God has many mysteries to his character. Like the lion Aslan in C. S. Lewis's *The Lion the Witch, and the Wardrobe* as discussed by Mr. Beaver and the children. The metaphoric Aslan wasn't safe, but he was the king of Narnia. Most importantly, he was good. This picture of God from a child's story reminds us that we cannot put the real Lord of the universe into a box. There are aspects to his character that will not be explained until the end of time.

Somehow though, God in his amazing way uses the pain of this fallen world with all its woes and sickness, the pain of when others hurt us, the pain of our own unsustainable plans, the pain of our mistakes and failures, to shape us and to shape our faith, to increase our hope for better days. Though my daughters are hurting, and David and I are hurting for them, I'm going to trust God for healing, for brighter futures as a family.

We're going to start looking for that celebration as David and I spend time with Lana praying together and—oh dear God—laughing together as we relinquish our child to him.

A South African Adoption—the Adoption of Susan
"A Grandfather's Story"
by birth family grandfather Charles Middleton

In 1977, following a yearlong furlough in Louisiana, our family returned to Malawi, a small southern African country, for a third missionary term. Our daughter Vicki, seventeen, and son Carl, sixteen, soon departed for missionary boarding school in Kenya, fifteen hundred miles away.

A few weeks into the school term my wife Glenda and I received a call from our daughter that was destined to alter all of our lives.

Tearfully Vicki said, "Mama and Daddy, I'm going to have a baby, and I can't stay at school. I have to come home."

"Vicki," I said, "we love you, and we are going to be with you through this experience. The main thing now is to get you home."

Of course, we were devastated. How would this affect Vicki's future? Would we be asked to return to the States and end our missionary service in Africa? What would be the response of our missionary colleagues and national Christians? But those matters were secondary. Our primary focus had to be Vicki's welfare.

Soon after Vicki's arrival back in Malawi we sat for prayer and discussion. "Vicki, you're a mature young lady with common sense. This is going to be your baby. We are not going to make any decisions about your future or the baby's. We won't override any decisions you make as long as they are not way off base. You can keep the baby and we will help you. Or you can put the baby up for adoption."

Neither Vicki nor her mother and I ever discussed or even considered abortion. Ultimately Vicki decided that, even with our help, trying to raise a child in a third-world country, as a seventeen-year-old, was unwise. A grandchild could not be covered by our Board's insurance, and we could not afford it on our limited salary. Vicki also felt it was essential that she get a college education in the States.

Our mission family and national coworkers were extremely understanding and supportive. A compassionate mission administrator in South Africa found a Christian maternity home in Cape Town where Vicki could have her baby. Our daughter was able to stay with us in Malawi for several months before departing for South Africa.

What I remember is that "our little girl" was going away for the most traumatic experience of her life, and her mom and dad couldn't go with her. That was torment! A flight from our home to Cape Town would take several hours and was far too expensive for us to visit her on our budget. We consoled ourselves that she was strong, healthy, and depending on the Lord. Glenda and I prayed for her twenty-four/seven.

We had not realized that an Afrikaans-speaking Christian organization operated the maternity home where Vicki would stay for the rest of her pregnancy. Of course, the staff spoke both Afrikaans, the language spoken by the descendants of Dutch settlers, and English, but we assumed that the baby would likely be adopted by an Afrikaans family and that we might never know what had happened to this precious baby. Vicki stressed that she wanted her baby to go to a Christian family, and the loving staff assured her that they shared her goal.

Occasionally we were able to phone her internationally. And finally, after she had borne a tiny baby girl and signed papers allowing for her adoption, she came home to Malawi and completed her senior year by homeschooling.

Twenty-one years later Vicki had earned a master's degree and worked as a clinical dietitian in a large Louisiana hospital. Her devoted Christian husband knew her adoption story, and they had two beautiful young daughters.

Glenda, especially, had continued to pray for the child of her child and asked the Lord to bless her and give her an abundant life. Glenda and I had transferred to the tiny mountain kingdom of Lesotho in Southern Africa in the early 1990s, but Glenda had been killed in a tragic automobile accident in 1995. I had since remarried. Rebecca, now serving with me in Lesotho, had, along with her late husband

Dudley, been a missionary colleague in Malawi, and Dudley had died of leukemia.

We received several phone calls from a Mrs. Marais in Cape Town, but each time she called, I was away. When I returned the calls, she was never in. One day when I was out shopping for mission supplies, Mrs. Marais called again. Rebecca encouraged her to leave a message so she could pass it on to me.

Mrs. Marais hesitantly said that she was seeking Vicki's contact information, and Rebecca replied that she could not comply without knowing the purpose. When Mrs. Marais said, "I understand that you are Mr. Middleton's second wife, and—" *Ah-ha!* A light went on in Rebecca's head, and she assured the caller that if it concerned Vicki's baby, she knew all about it and had gone through the situation with the Middletons. She heard an audible sigh of relief.

"This child, Susan," Mrs. Marais said, "is now twenty-one, and she wants to contact her birth mother. She was reared in a home of your same denomination here in Cape Town, is in university here, and is married to a young minister."

Imagine my joy when Rebecca greeted me with such a message. I immediately called Mrs. Marais, but because of the time difference had to wait a few hours to get Vicki on the phone in the early morning hours before she went to work.

Rebecca's eldest daughter, Melanie, had already planned to visit us in a few months. She and Vicki, now stepsisters, had grown up together in Malawi and were already fast friends. The two of them made plans to travel together, and we would meet them in Cape Town.

Correspondence, most of it by email, began to cram inboxes in Lesotho, the United States, and Cape Town. Susan's mother, Sheila, a lady of great warmth and humor, and her husband Edwin made arrangements at a bed and breakfast near their home so Vicki, Melanie, Rebecca, and I would be close and comfortable.

Rebecca and I made the long drive from Lesotho and arrived at the bed and breakfast Sunday evening before Vicki and Melanie were to arrive at the airport the next morning. We called Sheila and Edwin, and within five minutes they, Susan, and Susan's husband JeanRay joined us in our room, laughing and hugging us as though we were old friends.

The next morning we all went to the airport.

15

INHERITANCE

Christine, 2010 and 2011

Over the next couple of years as I watch Lana gradually grow stronger under excellent medical care, I delight in the happiness that she shows a little more each and every day. I love to go clothes shopping with Lana—she's as tall and slender as a model, and with her strong, quirky dark brows and hair tied back in a messy bun, at a quick glance she reminds people of Kate Middleton. Lana's even working in our church as a youth leader.

The boys, now young men, are involved in church too, especially Robert as a musician. Whatever interests my kids have, David and I are totally enamored with that subject. If it's Kyle's mechanics—though I don't really understand—I am also enamored by gadgets and gears. I'm in love with history, literature, and travel, because Lana is, and I'm in love with guitars because Robert loves leading others in worship music.

As time goes by, Kyle marries Crystal, a young woman with a baby from a previous relationship and who's been hurt badly through that abandonment. I know without being told that she is as emotionally bruised by her past as I was. Kyle's sensitive heart wants to love and protect Crystal and her little boy, Zechariah. *So that's what his boyish mind figured out so long ago when he'd gone out to the garage to tinker.* His mechanical mind pondered hard and long on his mom's experience of being pregnant and unmarried, and giving up her baby. I'm proud of my son for putting his faith into action, and for loving Crystal and Zech as his own.

As my family increases with Kyle's family of Crystal, Zech, and then two new grandsons Keenan and Micah, I'm reminded of the verses from Psalms 127 and 128 that I'd secretly underscored in the little white Bible I sent along with Sarah when she was a baby.

For a long time I thought of only the second verse, Psalm 128:6: "Yea, thou shalt see thy children's children," and I thanked God for giving me my three kids and for allowing me to "see" Sarah in my life. But for the first time Psalms 127:3 stands out for me. "Lo, children are an heritage of the LORD: and the fruit of the womb is his reward." The fruit of the womb is God's reward! *I am such a wealthy woman.* To me, my grown children and grandchildren are all strong young trees, growing sturdy and more fruitful each year with good deep roots.

It's at this time that I take a leap of faith and leave my job at Trinity Western to pursue my writing career full time. A number of opportunities present themselves—one of the most exciting is a ten-day missionary trip. All my kids have gone on short-term mission trips, serving various groups of suffering people around the world, and now it's my turn. The only difference is, as I join the group of other interested Christians on a visit to the south of India, I'll be serving Children's Camps International in a journalistic sense.

Seeing the vibrant, spice-scented subcontinent is a dream come true. Since I was a kid and read a number of books on the adventures of various missionaries who served in India, the country has enchanted me. Two of my favorites are the great American missionary Dr. Ida Scudder and Pandita Ramabai, a fascinating Indian Christian woman who in the past century developed a mission called *Mukti* that cared for poor cast-off women and orphans.

Now here, my feet planted on the dark-red soil of India, I am so grateful to God the Father for allowing me to feed this aspect of my true personality—a person entranced by the beauty of other cultures, by history, and most especially by India's search for God. In many of the places our missionary group visits, I see poverty, filth, and yet such beauty. In my spirit, I feel the Lord's yearning to draw them—especially the suffering women and children—into a close relationship with him.

Ten days whiz by, and before our group is due to fly home, we stop by a silk sari shop. A bolt of turquoise material studded with a heavy tapestry of amber beading—fit for a bride—calls to me. What possible use would I have for something so frivolous? I don't even sew. But the shopkeeper holds it out for me to touch. I move the silky fabric between my fingers. Such an exotic thing that doesn't match my North American style. I'd never be able to wear it. But as my finger traces the amber glass beading in a swirling Indian motif, I sense God's nudge to buy it on a whim of faith, to trust that he has sparkling things in store for us as a family.

The second exciting opportunity is WhiteFire Publishing wants to publish my book *Shadowed in Silk*. As my debut novel is about to be released, my publisher e-mails me with a selection of photos of various models for the front cover. I peruse the photos of these pretty women and smile. Funny how every single model resembles Sarah in some way. I'd not written my fictional character to look like my birth-daughter, but here are fuzzy images of her. On another whim I e-mail WhiteFire with photos of Sarah, suggesting her as the model for the front cover.

With my editor's happy agreement, and Lana's excited encouragement, I quickly e-mail Sarah asking her if she'd like to be the model for *Shadowed in Silk*. For the last few years, our e-mails to each other have increased from only one or two per year to now one every few months. Every Mother's Day she faithfully phones me. Each year that gift of her voice on that day floors me with gratitude. These last few years, on the day after Christmas, Sarah and Mark have met with our family for brunch or breakfast. Maybe she'll get a kick out of being the model for my book.

At first Sarah feels too shy, but her husband Mark talks her into it. A few weeks later we set up the photoshoot at our house, and Sarah and Mark make the long drive up from Washington. I'm nervous as I greet them at the door, worrying I've put Sarah on the spot. But here she is! Lana is at work, and I wish she were here as Sarah graciously accepts the costumes I've put together. She tries on first the typical English woman's outfit of 1919, a long linen skirt, white blouse, and straw boater hat.

I assume it's better if I leave Sarah and Mark alone with our photographer and remain upstairs, fearing my presence will only make her uncomfortable. After our photographer takes a few hundred photos of Sarah, in that costume, I creep down to the family room to see how things are progressing. To my dismay, I see that Sarah is having a hard time relaxing, and the stances for the photos are not as fluid as I envisioned.

As I enter the room I catch Sarah's eye, I realize my presence is not unwelcome at all. I swoop in and guide Sarah into moving around like a model to find the fluidity for the front cover that I imagine. We always seem to communicate better when the focus is not at all on our relationship but on the here and now.

We laugh while pretending to be professional models, and Sarah visibly relaxes in the outfit and straw boater hat as she holds up the sari material as if to inspect it in an Indian bazaar. While the poses aren't the stuff of glamor magazines, she's charmed by the beauty of the heavy amber beading. Her delight over the sari affirms our mutual love for the variety of cultures in God's world, and our photographer snaps the photos.

As Sarah changes into the sari a little later, she opens the bathroom door and with a breezy laugh, blows her hair away from her mouth, and whispers, "The top, the blouse is way too tight."

Between the two of us we manage to squeeze her into the sari blouse, and I pull it together at the back with a large safety pin. For the first time my heart sings with this genuine closeness with her. And good gracious, we're actually having fun.

When the book comes out several months later, I figure, *Well, this is it*! This is what God has been cultivating all along. My heavenly Father took my heartache over Sarah, through my journaling turned it into a muse, and now put her beautiful face on the front cover. And what a beautiful cover it is.

I'm happy. I can't remember the last time I cried, and my family is doing reasonably well. Lana is blossoming, doing a little travelling. So too are my sons flourishing. Kyle begins an apprenticeship in a mechanic's shop, and Robert obtains his degree in Worship Music from Briercrest College and Seminary. David and I watch with a deep well of satisfaction as our three children work toward their God-inspired callings.

And I am a published author. So this is the *me* that God has been growing all along. I've even begun to venture out as a motivational speaker at women's events. But another journey hovers on the horizon. This time though, it's not another canyon of pain that

I've dreaded. This time as a family we're set for a mountaintop experience, that sparkling celebration of joy I've been praying for.

That joy walks into our life in the form of a young man called James, whom Lana met at a Bible study. On a number of occasions James and Lana had argued over theological points. When Lana shares this with me, about that annoying guy in the Bible study, I feel my left brow arch upward and my ears perk. *She's all in a dither over a theological disagreement?* A few weeks later she introduces James to us. While feeling the calm, masculine strength of James's handshake, I take in his kind gaze that morphs into a cheeky twinkle when something humorous is said, usually by him. I know instantly this man is strong enough to protect Lana, tender enough to cherish her, and funny enough to make her laugh.

Their wedding a year later is everything I've ever prayed for my girl, a day of smiles and laughter. Lana is breathtaking as she glides down the aisle in a frothy gown of white organza on her dad's arm. And I think of Hans and Sarah, how good God has been to these two daughters of mine, to have such adoring dads. The immediate family wedding photos include David and me, and all my children—Lana and James, Robert, Kyle and Crystal and our grandsons...and Mark and Sarah. My joyful heritage from the Lord is increasing exponentially.

Around the same time, *Shadowed in Silk* wins some critical acclaim, and I'm hard at work on the second book of that series, *Captured by Moonlight.* For this cover I want Lana as the model, and WhiteFire designs a 1920s flapper dress for her. I'm overjoyed that my two exquisite daughters are what I've always felt in my heart—matching bookends. What more could I want? And I'm excited about this novel, setting it in the south of India where I actually visited the year before.

While in India I rode the same railways, walked in the footsteps of some of my favorite real-life missionaries from the turn of the twentieth century. Though I didn't visit the part of India where Pandita Ramabai built her *Mukti* mission, I've written a portion of my book to feature the ministry begun by that vibrant Indian Christian so many years ago. In this novel the romance of India acts as a backdrop for another spiritual lesson that I've learned—dying to one's own agenda.

One of my fictional Indian characters, Eshana, is the metaphor for this principle by portraying the same relinquishment (or death to my own agenda) that I've learned. It's my prayer that when I go through any future sorrow that I will have the faith and courage of Eshana when she says in my novel, "I will sing your praises, Lord. Though you have dressed me in funeral clothes, I will sing your praises with joy."

I'm in the midst of working on the final chapters of *Captured by Moonlight* when Sarah and Mark phone, happiness brimming in their voices. They're planning to visit us and share some news.

A few days later I greet Sarah and Mark in our small front foyer and exchange hugs. The hugs from both of them are as warm and genuine as mine when I reach up to embrace them. I recognize the feel of their touch in the same way I recognize my favorite rose when it blooms each June in my garden. Though I only see it for a season, I know its fragrance well, and I know its needs.

I lead them into the living room where a square dance of sorts begins with more hugging between them and David and Lana and James, and I note Mark and Sarah have hardly changed since their wedding thirteen years ago. Both are exceptional ER nurses in the States and remain tall and slender in their builds, and Sarah still looks every bit twenty-years-old rather than her thirty-three.

As the square dance of hugging ebbs, conversations erupt with the same noisy din that flavors all my children's gatherings. James and Mark are yacking up a storm as they sit close together at the ends of two different sofas, and Lana and Sarah are chatting just as vigorously from the far ends of the room. David beams as he interjects jokes into the two different conversations. In the kitchen nearby, I listen as I put a tray of drinks together, not needing to add a word. I glow on the inside like the gentle June sunshine on my rose garden, though I hope none of my old maternal neediness for Sarah shows. Nice and easy does it, I rcmind myself.

Once I'm satisfied everyone's comfortable and has a glass of something cold, I catch Sarah's eye and smile. "Are you going to tell us about your plans?"

Sarah's eyes smile as she sends me a brisk nod. The eruption of chatter in the room simmers down.

Together Mark and Sarah share their desire to work full time with Global Aid Network and present the mission as the rest of us listen intently. Their voices ring with energy as they explain how they're not going out like traditional missionaries to live on the foreign field but will do the administrative work here in Canada and fly to various parts of the world frequently throughout the year. In a medical capacity they will maintain standards for the care of widows and orphans in developing countries. If they receive enough pledges for financial support, they'll start with Sarah working for GAiN first, and Mark will follow.

A flash of that poor woman I used to identify with passes before my eyes. She, sitting in the dust, hungry, forgotten, and holding out her baby, fills me with sadness. But here, with God's help, there is hope that poor woman will find the same joy and peace as I have found.

Sarah edges forward on the sofa, her eyes bright, as if she's leaning as far into our family clutch as possible. My soul dances that she's finally becoming the missionary nurse she's always dreamed of being. Here too is God's work in a relinquished life, when God is allowed to work through the DNA of the person he's created.

I watch her excitement as she and Mark discuss which video to load on our TV so we can see the orphanages around the world that she'll be working with. I sense her inability to remain static a moment longer as she leaves the polite constriction of the sofa and perches on her knees between the fireplace and TV. Her hands flutter through the presentation materials to choose which DVD is best. Her smile comes so readily, and a growing exhilaration sparks in me. She's making herself at home...in my home, with not a hint of reserve as the short film begins.

Still on her knees, she rests back on her haunches but leans up and forward each time she points out something on the TV. She settles back with a smile to watch the slides of children and outlines how GAiN's Women and Children's ministry works in partnership with other organizations. And I catch a new understanding in her tone. She knows that we care about her service to God not just because this is such a worthy missionary undertaking but because we are family.

Whenever her open gaze connects with mine, something fizzes along my bloodstream. I know her. The pixels of that ghostly image of a girl I met at the reunion in 1999 have developed before my eyes. Just as it says in 1 Corinthians 13, for a long time we could see each other in a mirror dimly, but now we are seeing each other face-to-face. Right now, Sarah and I still only know each other in part, but one day I will know Sarah fully as I also will be fully known to her. The same for all of us when we get to heaven, to be known and loved by God, and by one another.

"I'll be working with orphanages in Taiwan, Vietnam, and Haiti, to name a few," Sarah adds with raised brows and a happy exhale. "And the Ramabai Mukti Mission in India."

That fizzing in my bloodstream rises up like a geyser in my chest. While she goes on to explain her goal to defend the rights of the fatherless and the weak and the poor, I push out a breath in a rush of adrenaline, and give one loud clap of my hands and laugh.

Sarah looks at me with a little grin, a half-knowing look in her eyes. "I think I remember now. You know about the *Mukti*, don't you?"

"Yes." My pulse leaps like a hysterical rabbit. "I've been interested in that mission for years. In fact, a portion of the book I'm currently writing features the *Mukti*."

She gives me a wide, uninhibited smile, complete with the shared knowledge that God has entwined both of our callings—me as a writer and her as a nurse—for this one shining moment in time, upon this one mission in India...of all the missions in all the world.

That bond with Sarah I have wanted for so long is here at last. Not the bond of mother and babe that I lost and strove to get back. This bond is brand new for us, but it resembles to a smaller extent the bond I share with my other children, that shared interest in what God is growing in them. My maternal love for Sarah that I've never known what to do with now has an avenue to flow upon, just as it does for Lana, Kyle, and Robert.

After their presentation, Mark and Sarah stay for a while to visit. The three men find things to talk about so easily, and frankly I pay their conversation little heed. Sitting across from my two daughters, my soul swells in quiet peace as they sink back against my couch cushions, drinking tea. They also ignore the men's boring discussion of cars, video games or...whatever.

Lana and Sarah focus on far more interesting girl stuff: their work, clothes, cats, marriage, favorite books.

"I love the biography *Bonhoeffer: Pastor, Martyr, Prophet, Spy* by Eric Metaxas," says Lana. "One of the best written biographies ever! And Corrie ten Boom's books are a staple in my life." She waves a hand as she thinks back. "And oh yeah, *A Thousand Splendid Suns* by Khaled Hosseini."

"Oh, great books," Sarah agrees, her eyes as wide as Lana's. "You like some light reading too?"

"I'm a big fan of fantasy," Lana goes on. "You can't be part of our family and not be. You know, the usual, C. S. Lewis, Tolkien, and Mom introduced me to The Dragonriders of Pern series when I was a kid so that lately I've been devouring the *Fionavar Tapestry* that evolve into dragon stories."

Sarah nods. "There's definitely a place for different weight in books. I've recently re-read Elisabeth Elliot's *Through Gates of Splendor*, but I also like to kick back with something lighter like Francine Rivers and have a laugh over one of the Shopaholic books. They're just so funny."

I don't want to add a word as I savor the comfort and intimacy blossoming right in front of me. As a family we've gone through a new set of doors this evening. I fancy that I'm walking through open glass panels out to a sunlit garden where the flowers are in full bloom. When Mark and Sarah prepare to leave, the square dance of hugs starts over again, and we all squeeze into the stairwell above our small foyer to say goodbye. Outside on the front porch, David, Lana, James, and I wave until Sarah and Mark have driven off.

After they're gone, as Lana cuddles beside James in the living room and talks to her dad, I clean up the kitchen and think back to those long tearful nights when I was pregnant with Sarah. Those nights when I'd prayed on my knees, my arms around my tummy to protect my baby from the stress I was undergoing. Back then I wondered if my emotions, especially my depression but also my prayers, would affect my child's personality. I wondered too if something of my growing faith at that time would be passed through to my baby during those long sessions on my knees. As I imagine Sarah and Mark driving away from our house to go and stay over at her mom's place tonight, I want to believe that in a spiritual sense, some of what Sarah is today was seeded in my prayers.

And I think of Anne and Hans. It wasn't just their daughter's heart I saw tonight but also theirs. Anne and Hans have virtually been here in my home, in that the results of Anne's mothering and Hans's fathering are so visible to me. Their parenting is such a thing of beauty.

I remember again those verses I'd underlined in Sarah's little white Bible. Having underlined two verses in Psalms, I'd fixated only on the one of "seeing" my children. I'd forgotten that I underlined that other verse about children being an inheritance from the Lord. Perhaps that silly coded message in Sarah's Bible wasn't meant for her at all, because though I'd forgotten, God had not. My children and grandchildren are such a wonderful harvest God is reaping, part of my inheritance from him.

A South African Adoption—the Adoption of Susan

"A Unique Family"

By adoptive mother Sheila Callanan, birth mother Vicki Blackwell, and grandfather Charles Middleton

Sheila: As Edwin and I, our two daughters and their husbands, and Charles and Rebecca waited at the airport on Monday, September 6, 1999 for the KLM flight to land, Susan and I both knew that in a few moments our lives could not be the same again. I reflected on my own private thoughts and so did Susan. Slowly people filed out through customs, and then I saw her...the girl who had given my child life. God had chosen us to teach her how to live. We went forward to greet her, Susan ahead. Tears filled our eyes as we stood back—adoptive family, Susan's husband, biological grandfather, and step-mom—and we all watched Vicki touching and seeing her child for the first time. Her first words were, "You are so beautiful."

The Callanan family had increased through the marriages of our two daughters, giving Edwin and me two sons-in-*love*. Linda was busy studying for her doctorate in chemical engineering while Susan was majoring in psychology at the Cornerstone Institute.

Frustrations and delays had marked our reunion journey to this point. Six long months ago we received the details about Susan's grandparents. Though Grandpa Charles wanted so many more facts, the social worker preferred her mother be the first to hear. Charles gave them her address, and the society wrote Vicki a long letter containing information about Susan.

Charles phoned the social worker about the delay, but the letter never made it to Vicki in Louisiana. At the time, we didn't know this. Susan's anxiety rose as she worked through the possibility that maybe her mother didn't want to meet her. Through those six months of waiting she again reached the place of confirmation in her heart that her identity rested in Christ and she would be the same person whether she met her mother or not.

We too phoned the adoption society, asking if they had heard anything. They phoned the United States and discovered their letter had never arrived. They then decided that Susan could go ahead and send an e-mail directly to her mother, along with the photo of Susan in her sari. What feelings must have gone through her mother's mind as she saw a picture of her daughter? Edwin and I also phoned her grandparents to introduce ourselves.

September arrived at last. Susan's mother arranged to fly to South Africa. And she didn't have to fly alone, another miracle in God's big plan. Vicki's stepsister would be a wonderful support at this emotional time. Grandpa Charles had already planned to drive down to Cape Town to pick up the sister before he knew that his daughter would be coming as well. We were therefore blessed not only to meet Susan's mother but other members of her biological family.

Vicki: At the Cape Town airport, Susan, her husband Jean-Ray, her parents Sheila and Edwin, her sister Linda and brother-in-law Eric, as well as Dad and Rebecca, met us. Meeting Susan, hugging her, and seeing a face that had for so long just been in my imagination was surreal.

We celebrated that whole week. We met extended family and church friends, laughed and talked while walking the sandy beaches, and were together daylight to dark.

Both Susan and I have quieter personalities. Sheila made it easy to interact because she was so jovial and outgoing. Obviously secure in her role as Susan's mother, she and Edwin—who is also a bit quiet like Susan and me—seemed perfectly at ease in accepting another whole family. Because of all the e-mails that had passed among everyone prior to our meeting, I had no apprehension that there would be any strained relationships.

One thing Sheila did early on put us at ease—she exclaimed,

"Look, you and Susan have the same feet!" We also noted that we had the same hands. Susan and I, like my mother and all of her sisters, have very small hands and feet.

One day as Susan and I walked together some distance in front of Sheila and Rebecca, Sheila nudged Rebecca and laughed. "Look at those two. They look like sisters walking there."

Grandpa Charles: What a reunion we had! It wasn't just Susan and Vicki who cried when they embraced. We all wept with joy!

Originally we planned to have a couple of meals together with Susan's folks and to allow much private time for Vicki and Susan to get to know each other. It didn't work that way.

For the next week ALL of us were together almost constantly. We shopped, ate, visited, went to tourist sites, spent time with Susan's older sister Linda and her husband Eric, and enjoyed supper at the home of JeanRay's parents.

Our first day together the whole gang gathered at the bed and breakfast. Vicki and I stood talking to each other, and Susan passed between us on the way to another room.

Vicki and I looked at each other with our eyes wide and our mouths open. Susan looked so much like Glenda! She even walked like her! How gratifying it was to know that her grandmother, who she would never meet this side of heaven, lived on in her. Later I gave Susan Glenda's seSotho Bible, which had been in the car with her the day she died.

Vicki: Since our reunion we've remained in touch with Susan and her family, by phone and e-mail, and have had several visits back and forth across the oceans. Our families have developed a deep spiritual bond. ALL of us had prayed for one another for years, even though we didn't know who the others were or where they lived.

When I remember meeting Susan, I am awed that I walked into such a dramatic and exciting situation but somehow felt it was always meant to be. I continue to be overcome by the beautiful relationship that started out with love and continues to grow. I think God meant it to be that way for his glory.

Joel 2:12-14 has a special meaning to me in the "Susan story." Long ago I gave the situation to the Lord but didn't expect anything special to happen. But twenty years later he let me know that this precious baby was alive and healthy, that she had been reared by godly parents, and that she had had a truly blessed life. We have not only been able to meet, but to become one big family.

> "Even now," declares the Lord, "return to me with all your heart, with fasting and weeping and mourning." Rend your heart and not your garments. Return to the Lord your God, for he is gracious and compassionate, slow to anger and abounding in love, and he relents from sending calamity. Who knows? He may turn and relent and leave behind a blessing—grain offerings and drink offerings for the Lord your God."

At the end of our five days, I left this note for Sheila to find after I left Cape Town.

> Dear Sheila,
>
> I guess I have a better understanding of how Mary felt (Luke 2:19) when she, "treasured up all these things and pondered them in her heart." This has all been so amazing for me. I would sometimes imagine about hearing from my child, but this has exceeded

> all I ever imagined. Only God has the capacity to do that. Ephesians 3:20, one of my favorite verses, says, "Now to Him who is able to do exceedingly abundantly above all that we ask or think, according to the power that works in us, to Him *be* glory in the church by Christ Jesus to all generations, forever and ever. Amen" (NKJV).

Grandpa Charles: Since that eventful week in Cape Town, Sheila and Edwin have visited us several times in Louisiana, where we retired after thirty-two years in Africa. Edwin always brings work clothes and does repairs and projects at our house. We have been to New Orleans, Branson, Nashville, and the Texas Hill Country together. Susan and Jean-Ray have been here several times as well, and we were thrilled whenever they and their three children (they now have four!) were able to be with our whole family for Christmas. At the end of 2014 the South African folks all returned again to Louisiana for New Year. We are never out of touch, thanks to cheaper international calling and e-mails.

I have often thought of that passage from Romans 8:28 that says, "And we know that all things work together for good to them that love God, to them who are the called according to his purpose" (KJV).

God took a crushing experience of many years ago and transformed it into a glorious outcome through redemption, growth in grace, an answer to prayer for a young couple hungry for a baby, and a joining together of two loving Christian families.

Sheila: We fell in love with them all at our reunion and knew from that moment that our two families would become a unique blended one. The memories of those days are ingrained in our minds forever. While we spent time with Charles and Rebecca and their daughter, Susan and Vicki spent one-on-one time with each other. And as we spoke and shared we could see the threads of God's tapestry being woven together to make this beautiful picture that we were now part of.

Up until now we had only seen the back of the tapestry. The more we chatted the more we saw little miracles that happened over the years. Our reunion answered the prayers from many years before—prayers of faith knowing that the answers may never be seen on earth.

The following is part of a letter I wrote to Susan's mother before she came to South Africa. I wanted her to know that her coming here was fine with us. In some ways we had prepared for this for twenty-one years.

> Dear Vicki,
>
> I am not sure how one ever expresses gratitude to a person for making a sacrifice that brought the most unbelievable joy to a family. All I can say is thank you from the bottom of my heart. I believe that people have the capacity to love many people in different ways—not overlapping but side by side, each one having a different relationship. Because of this belief, I share Susan with you. When I refer to you as Susan's mother sometimes people do not always understand, and they argue that I am her mother. I don't expect them to understand. For me, Susan has two mothers.

Three months after our adoption reunion, Susan and our family also met Susan's biological father. He flew to Cape Town from the United States.

Vicki made it as easy as possible for Susan to make contact with her father. Vicki made every effort to find out where he was, she never mentioned that it was hard for her, and she only thought of Susan at that time.

As I write, we are planning once again to visit America. Are we visiting family? Of course we are—a very unique one. We have been many times. On Susan's second visit she traveled alone and happened to be in the United States during the 9/11 attack. Quite an anxious time for us back in South Africa. Vicki has been able to come out and visit Susan and Jean-Ray at their home in Durban, where they now live on the east coast of South Africa, about a two-hour flight from Cape Town. Jean-Ray is one of the pastors at a large Baptist Church in Westville, Durban. And this past winter of 2016, Vicki travelled again to visit Susan alone, and I rejoiced over their chance to grow closer.

After all these years our home is filled with the sounds of children. Susan and her three children, Camilla, Aren, and Elissa, lived with us for a year while Susan did her honors in psychology. The cycle began again when Susan and Jean-Ray adopted their son Aren.

Thank you, to all those who walked this path of sweet memories with us. To those who have read our stories and remembered that you were part of them. You will always have a special place in our hearts.

And from one mother to another: "Vicki, I love you more than words can tell. John 16:22: "'So with you: Now is your time of grief, but I will see you again and you will rejoice, and no one will take away your joy.'"

16

A Child's Perspective

From Washington State—The Adoption of Sarah
"A Child's Perspective"
By adoptee, Sarah (VandenBos) Blaney

We serve a God who loves to take what is broken and restore it to its original design. Adoption is a beautiful picture of God's redemption of his creation. I can say with all honesty that I love the fact that I am an adopted child. However, this complex relationship brings blessing and pain for everyone involved. Adoption is only needed because we live in a broken world where things do not go according to God's original plan. So while I am thankful to be adopted, I am reminded of the heartache and loss for every person involved in the relationship: the child, the parents, and the birth family.

Growing up I frequently thought of my birth mom. I don't think I fantasized like some adopted children do, imagining their mom or dad to be some wonderful, perfect, superhero parent. I was more curious about her personality, her appearance, what traits I inherited from relatives. Since my physical characteristics were quite different from everyone else in my immediate family, I had a strong need to belong by sharing those traits with my birth family. Our closed adoption prohibited me from pursuing a meeting with them until I turned nineteen. Always supportive, my mom assured me if I ever desired to meet my birth mother, she would help me.

As a child, I grew up confident in my parents' love. Although not perfect—no parent is—they frequently reminded me how much they cherished me. For this I am eternally grateful. I believe my view of God as a loving Father is a direct result of having loving parents. My mom and dad spoke highly of my brothers' and my birth parents, honored them, and prayed for them. They talked about my adoption openly and in a positive light. They helped me realize that adoption is something to be proud of, not ashamed of. However, there was always a missing puzzle piece in the picture of my life. Always that one unknown. A happy person with all my needs met, I still wondered about my birth family.

When Christine contacted me asking to meet, initially my emotions took a roller-coaster ride. Excited, nervous, fearful. Most of all, great responsibility for the feelings and pain of all involved weighed on me. I wanted to honor my parents and respect their wishes. As supportive as my mom tried to be, I could tell it was difficult for her. She graciously encouraged me in whatever decision I made, but through eyes full of tears. My dad, however, was crushed. He did not understand why I would need to meet my birth family. Regardless of our not being blood-related, I was fully his. Even though nothing could be further from the truth, I think for him meeting my birth family felt like a betrayal.

The reunion also came at a busy season of life as I approached year-end nursing school exams, volunteering, working part time, and preparing for a wedding. In less than a month, I was to marry my high-school sweetheart. Holding the letter from Christine in my hand, I prayed for wisdom. "Lord, how do I accomplish all this? How do I navigate these tumultuous emotions of demanding school courses, getting married, and now potentially meeting my birth mother?" As my mom and I talked, we considered waiting until the summer, during school break, and after the wedding. However, she suggested that perhaps it would mean a lot to Christine if she could be present to see me married. Although it gave me a very short time to emotionally prepare for the reunion, I agreed.

The reunion was surreal in some ways. I finally came face-to-face with a blood relative who I resembled! My lack of strong emotions during the reunion surprised me. In many ways, she was a stranger, as if I was meeting someone new. Also, with all the major life transitions occurring almost simultaneously, I think I guarded my heart and remained in survival mode. While the reunion satisfied my longings and curiosity regarding my birth family, I sensed Christine's disappointment in how our relationship looked. I really did try to be like a daughter to the best of my ability, but tapped out emotionally and physically, I knew what I was offering was not quite enough. I remember that time as being very weighty.

My personality is to please, and I desperately wanted to keep all parties happy. Yet I knew I failed on every front. I felt a responsibility toward my birth mom, Lana, my parents, Mark, and his family. I wanted to pursue a sister-like relationship with Lana but had no idea where or how to start that. I didn't know Lana's expectations or desires.

Over the years following the reunion, I knew I disappointed Christine. Our relationship did not resemble what she hoped for. But I felt stuck and emotionally spent. Eventually our relationship settled into something peaceful where we now enjoy connecting as close extended family.

For as long as I could remember, two life goals stood out: be a nurse serving as a missionary and be a mother. With these single-minded goals, I entered nursing school straight out of high school. My husband also pursued a career in nursing, and we spent the next years thriving in the field. I loved my job, and it came easily to me. But a desire burned deep within me to serve the Lord full time with my nursing gifts. My husband and I took every opportunity to serve in short-term medical missions all over the world, and I found myself constantly researching medical mission organizations.

Finally, after years of research and prayer, the prospect of working with Global Aid Network in Canada presented itself. This humanitarian aid organization dedicated to "demonstrating the love of God, in word and deed, to hurting and needy people around the world through relief and development projects," fit perfectly. In all honesty, not until I recently re-read some of my old journals did I realize this was indeed an answer to prayer. So bogged down in the realities of everyday life, I had forgotten to ever *ask* God to serve him in this way. Thankfully, he showed he is always listening and answering prayers, even when I forget to pray them.

In regards to being a mother, that has been an interesting journey. A few years into marriage, my husband and I started trying to have children. We did not presume we would have any difficulties bearing a child. We were young and overall healthy. After a few months we became pregnant but eight weeks later we miscarried. We told ourselves, and others told us, "Don't worry, that often happens the first time. The next pregnancy will be different."

It wasn't. Neither was the next or the one after and so on.

The following years turned into a blur of fertility testing and loss. Our hopes soared every time a small gummy bear became visible on the ultrasound machine, then shattered when they could detect no heartbeat. We lost most of the babies during the first trimester of pregnancy. No physician could tell us definitively what was wrong. None of the tests revealed what caused the miscarriages. After one particularly bad experience where I lost so much blood I needed to be hospitalized, my husband and I decided we needed a break, a time away from the monitoring, testing, and disappointments.

During this season of rest, my heart stirred for adoption. As an adopted child, I always hoped I could also be an adoptive mom. My husband and I decided to pursue adopting a child or sibling group from the foster system. We went through all the training and preparation required. Ready and equipped, we could handle anything. It would be hard but so worth it!

A few months later, a nine-year-old girl and her six-year-old brother joined our family. Over the next month, we did our best to be loving parents to these hurting little children. However, we quickly saw we were in over our heads. We were not able to keep them safe. The level of trauma they had experienced in their short lives was much, much greater than any of the therapists and case managers realized. My husband and I made the heart-wrenching, guilt-laden decision to give them up to another family in the foster system.

As I sat there with empty arms again, I asked God, "How can I do this? How do I let them go?"

I felt God answer, "Do you think you can do a better job loving them than I can? You think you love them more than I do? Let them go and trust me that I have a better plan." I have had to go back to those words from God many, many times over the years as a reminder that I am not in control.

"'For my thoughts are not your thoughts, neither are your ways my ways,' declares the LORD. 'As the heavens are higher than the earth, so are my ways higher than your ways and my thoughts than your thoughts'" (Isaiah 55:8-9).

For months and years following, I walked through a desert wasteland, my heart heavy with grief, all hope of babies and children gone. Just when I thought I had cried all my tears, more gathered and fell. Darkness and thoughts of suicide plagued me. I wish I could say this was not the case. I wish I could say my joy triumphed in the midst of pain and my hope shone in a seemingly hopeless situation. But I cannot.

Through this time, I turned frequently to the Psalms. My soul resonated with David's brutal honesty with God, his crying out for God to heal him and deliver him from anguish. I found myself often on my knees reciting Psalms of God's promise to not abandon me. Although I struggled to accept the situation, my heart knew that God as a loving Father grieved alongside me. Many times I physically reached out and pictured Jesus holding my hand. I meditated on Hannah's prayer in the second chapter of 1 Samuel. Just like Hannah, I wept bitterly before the Lord and asked him to grant me a child.

The hardest part of the infertility and failed adoption was accepting my contribution in further traumatizing the children. In one of my journal entries, I cried out to God asking how he could have let me hurt those children. My husband and I going through multiple miscarriages was one thing to bear, but to bring children into our home with the promise to give them a forever home only to go back on that promise was, in my mind, inexcusable. I struggled to forgive myself. I thought, "Have I strayed so far off your path that the only way to get my attention was to let me further traumatize these children?"

Suddenly the cross and grace took on a whole new meaning. I always understood that Jesus went to the cross to pay the price, to take on the rejection of his Father all because of my sin. But now that truth carried an even greater weight in my heart. If God could still love me and forgive me through this then like it says in Romans 8:38, there is truly nothing that could separate me from the love of God.

I told God, "I have no hope, no joy, no faith. I need you to give it to me because there is nothing left in me."

It didn't happen overnight. But slowly, with the work of the Holy Spirit and the love and words of truth spoken by friends, my season of walking the desert ended. One day I realized that four days had passed since I last cried. Hope glimmered. Then a glimmer of joy. Then a glimmer of faith. Gifts given by the Holy Spirit I asked—no, begged—God for, sometimes every hour because I hated my emptiness. God heard my prayers and rescued me from the pit. As promised, he placed my feet on the solid rock of his steadfast love, and gratitude replaced my emptiness.

It has taken years to retrain my brain not to automatically operate like I was still suffering depression. When my thoughts want to go down a path of hopelessness, I remind myself of all that Jesus did for me and am filled with thankfulness instead. For the first time in many years, I could honestly say I was fully satisfied. No longer consumed with hurt and loss, I rested in the fact that, regardless of the future, I am deeply loved by God and I trust him completely.

Deep in my heart I held on to the hope that one day I would carry a child full-term. I was willing to continue pursuing a family despite the cost. My husband, however, did not want to take the risk. With the tumultuous adoption experience and multiple difficult, sometimes dangerous miscarriages, he did not have the emotional strength to try for a child. It took a few years, but he eventually acknowledged that God prompted him to try for a baby despite the risks.

A few months later, we found out we were pregnant. A week before Christmas I thought, "This is it. This pregnancy will last."

However, a few weeks later we miscarried. Heartbroken, I struggled to accept it and wondered what God was up to. Thankfully, a few months later, while traveling, we discovered that we were pregnant again. Guardedly excited this time, it was hard not to start every sentence with, "*If* this pregnancy lasts..." We hesitated to dream about the future or hope for the child since we knew all too well the possibility of miscarriage. We took each day cautiously, grateful for every moment that our little one still lived.

One day as I sat in the doctor's office waiting to be called in for our fifteen-week ultrasound, I realized my heart was racing. I checked my pulse. Over 120 beats per minute. I'd not even been aware of my anxiety! Suddenly it occurred to me—I had never left the doctor's office after a second ultrasound with a good report. None of my pregnancies made it past fifteen weeks. Even though I was not consciously thinking this, my heart knew.

Thankfully, that day we saw a heartbeat and I heard God tell me, "Everything is going to be fine. I am not promising that this pregnancy will go to full-term or that the baby will be okay after, but I am promising you that I am with you every step of the way."

A huge weight lifted off my shoulders, and I completely released the cares and worries to God. I never felt that same anxiety for the rest of the pregnancy. The following winter, we safely delivered a healthy, beautiful boy. His first name, Ian, means "God is gracious," and his second name, Samuel, means "God hears." Over the years, God has been so gracious to us when we deserved much, much worse. And he heard my cries.

What stands out to me so much more since the birth of my son is the truth of what Solomon wrote in Ecclesiastes. There is nothing in life that brings us pleasure other than God. "For without him, who can eat or find enjoyment?" (Ecclesiastes 2:25). God has answered my prayer for a child and he has fulfilled my dream of being a nurse overseas serving the least of these.

But the greatest gift he ever gave me is himself. His presence. His peace that surpasses understanding and love that has no end. I love my family, but they cannot come close to fulfilling the deep longings in my heart for God. He satisfies all our needs. Only Jesus is the ultimate rest (Hebrews 4), a thirst quenched forever (John 4), the true bread from heaven (John 6:33-35), and we can taste and see that the Lord is good (Psalm 34:8). Although I do not wish to repeat the years I walked through the desert in grief, I am eternally grateful for the gifts that came through that time. A deep, immoveable joy comes as a result of walking hand-in-hand with our Savior through suffering.

I cannot begin to understand why God works the way he does, but I do find it very interesting that my parents were married fifteen years before they received me, and my husband and I were married fifteen years before our son arrived. My mom and I shared the pain of heartache and barrenness as well as finding joy in the midst of pain. I find it also interesting that I have shared a similar pain as my birth mom in giving up a child—in my case, two children. All three women in our adoption triad experienced the pain of losing a child and learned to find satisfaction in God alone.

During the years after our reunion, I took on too much responsibility for the emotions of others. I took on the burden of my birth mother's unmet desires and disappointment; my birth sister Lana's struggles; and my brothers' and parents' inability to understand my need for a relationship with my birth family. Mark, always supportive, acted as my rock during that time, mostly because no one I knew had ever gone through an adoption reunion before. My mom was encouraging and caring about the reunion, but the reunion became a constant, painful reminder to her that she could not physically carry a child. Mindful of this, I tried to protect her as much as possible.

I guess I came across as distant to Christine, but I do not show much emotion and never have. That does not mean there isn't a torrent going on underneath. And when I am struggling to control my emotions, I get particularly quiet. So in the majority of my encounters with my birth mom I probably conducted myself more quietly than normal as I tried to sort through everyone's reactions and needs. I shielded in an attempt to protect people on every side.

I recognize my sin in it all now—those efforts to please people and not trusting that God is in control.

Our loving Daddy in heaven so delicately orchestrated all the events surrounding the adoption, our reunion, and our journey to becoming parents. In the midst of it, life is messy and painful. We are hurting people in a broken world. But with an eternal perspective, it is clear that our Father is at work bringing healing and redemption to a world he loves so dearly, and all the glory goes to him.

I no longer carry the amount of burden that I used to. And I have released my relationships with all my loved ones—my mom and brothers, my parents-in-law, and my birth family—to God and trust that the Holy Spirit will guide me. I am thankful for what the

Lord is doing in all of our lives these days. As I eagerly await the upcoming birth of our second son, I thank God for this season of life. It fills my heart with joy to see the gift that we have been given when Ian is held by one of his many grandmothers, aunts, and uncles whether through adoption, marriage, or biological lines.

God taught me through this journey that he is the true satisfaction of my soul. I am incredibly grateful for my son and my heart overflows with love for him, but I know that the love my Father has for me is even greater than the love I have for my child. As I watch him sleep I imagine God, my Father, similarly smiling on me with delight. God turned my mourning into dancing and gave me a garment of praise instead of a spirit of despair. However, he did that by changing my heart through the sacrifice of Jesus. It is not Ian or the son growing inside me who can provide that deep, true joy. The joy I speak of is a result of resting securely in my Father's arms, knowing I am seen and loved.

THE HARVEST by Christine

Time stopped for a few instances in my life. The day I met David, the day each of my babies were born and I held them in my arms. That day the gray steel elevator doors on the maternity ward closed. And the day I sneaked into a high school, as teenagers rushed through hectic halls and class bells receded to a muffled hush, and I found the grad photos that started with the letter V.

The clock stopped ticking the day I ran into an emergency ward, broken over the fact that my precious daughter, my girl, was too sad to want to live.

But time stopped, too, in a joyful way when my son Kyle introduced me to a diminutive young woman with curly red hair, pushing a cute blond toddler in a stroller. The day I met my son-in-*love* James, and his and Lana's happy, happy wedding. And the day I held each of my newborn grandsons, Keenan and Micah, and later, Ian and Ezra, Sarah's baby boys.

These days I am just like Naomi when she holds the child of Ruth and Boaz on her lap. No longer bitter Mara but pleasant Naomi.

Time comes to a sudden cessation each time another joy enters my life. Like the day my youngest son Robert phoned to say, "Hey, Mum...I've met someone." As of the writing of this book I'm over the moon with joy. In a few weeks Robert will marry Sara Ruiz—yes, another Sara—a beautiful Venezuelan and Spanish beauty who's won Robert's heart. I'm so looking forward to gaining some salsa in our family when the Ruiz family joins with ours in the marriage of our children. I'm just like the woman at the well, my cup of joy brims and runs over.

But as I near the closing of these chapters, I can't rest on my laurels and type "The End" just yet. None of us will be fully developed until we cross the Jordan from this world to the next and see God the Father face-to-face and run to his open arms. That's what my confused spirit was really looking for all along. Not Sarah, not me, but the Lord God. Like the name Ruth means *friend*, the deepest, most loving friendship I need is with my heavenly Father. In that regard, I am just like Abraham.

And today when I look at my birth daughter, delight seasons my prayers for her work on behalf of that poor third-world woman sitting in the dust, holding out her child. Just like Hannah in her song, I too rejoice. "He raises the poor from the dust, he lifts the needy from the ash heap to make them sit with nobles, and inherit a seat of honor...."

For a long time I wished I could turn the clock back and decide this time around not to relinquish her. But how can I love Sarah and even for a moment imagine her not in the loving family God arranged for her? I love her! So today I rejoice that I gave her up to her dad Hans and her mom Anne, and to her brothers Matthew and Luke.

Still, it does my heart good—no, it soars—when I read messages on Facebook from Sarah, like the one she posted on Mother's Day a few years ago. "I am so grateful for the moms in my life—my mom Anne, my birth mom Christine, and my mother-in-law Susan...." A wave of pride washes over me whenever Sarah introduces me as her birth mom to her friends.

And my heart soars just as much over my precious girl Lana. I'm seeing the real Lana too these days, a beautiful woman who loves God and her husband. Joy also overflows when Kyle and Crystal and the three boys clamor into our house for a loud, messy family meal with loads of shenanigans and a din that makes our ears ring. Or when I receive a poem like the following, written by Robert, who now lives a whole province away.

To Mum

Even before I knew what to call it,
you spoke Art into my life.
Your love was patience, struggle, passion, and vigor,
all at once...
showing me a daily shine.
You raised me in kingdom language.

You spoke the sort of grace that brings daisies to lift up their necks,
even in the face of an unkind wind.

~ Robert Campbell Schmidtke

When I look at my kids I remember what my mother always says. "Our children are only on loan to us for a while." Just like King David, as a family God helped us learn to forgive ourselves as we forgive others. As Lana forgives me for my failures as her mom, it brings a lightness to my soul I've not experienced since my own childhood. At our family get-togethers we've nurtured a strong disposition toward laughter, especially playing games at the kitchen table.

Looking back on the reunion, I affirm Hans's stand. He had every right to his emotions. I affirm Anne's stand too, of not integrating me into her private life, although the sweetest relationship from a slight distance ripened over the years.

Anne and I often e-mail each other, especially when Sarah presents her with a grandchild. We have spoken in person a number of times since the reunion. I sense her love for me, and she is effusive in her compliments, telling me how much she appreciates and admires me. That sentiment goes two ways. I'm embarrassed when I hear how often she tells her family and friends what a fine Christian I am. I'm glad this book can set the record straight on that score. I blush when I hear that Anne buys my books to give out as gifts to family and friends. And my joy skyrockets that at last my vision from so long ago, of Anne and I sharing our combined story, rests within the pages of this book.

Not all adoption reunions are the same. People are made up of such different emotional stuff. As for meeting Hans, I look forward to that day when I get to heaven too, and I'll seek him out and run to him with a big hug and call him brother. Because in heaven we will no longer see each other as a reflection in a dark mirror. We'll see each other face-to-face, know each other fully, and Hans will no longer fear me as a threat to his joy. Just like Mary, Martha, and Lazarus, when the Lord comforted them, so too are my brother Hans and I comforted.

Besides, God provided everything I ever dreamed of. As a lonely immigrant kid in Canada with most of my relatives on the other side of the ocean, and growing up with a neglectful dad, I've come to love Psalm 68:6. "God sets the lonely in families." And I know that the Lord will always see me, and always hear me, whenever I feel just like Hagar and enter a new desert of sadness.

Through my journey as a writer, I've gained friendships with David and Renée Sanford, Cathy West, a fellow fiction author, and Cheryl Unrau, who I met on my trip to India. But one of the most precious relationships is with my writing sister and critique partner, Rachel Phifer. For the purposes of writing this book, Rachel introduced me to another adoption reunion within her own family circle. Rachel is Rebecca's other daughter. Now I feel like kin to Charles and Rebecca in Louisiana, and Vicki and her family, as well as Sheila and Edwin, and Susan and Jean-Ray in South Africa. I can't wait for their next adoptive and birth family gathering, because David and I are showing up too. Hold a spot for us at the table.

I know who I am these days. In jest whenever I speak at women's events, I introduce myself as, "I'm a woman who, when I get to heaven, hopes to sing Gregorian chants with an Abbey of Irish monks, bang a tambourine with an African/American Baptist choir, and dance in a Bollywood musical, all to the glory of God. But I'm not really joking, I'm just laughing as I speak the truth." Besides, now I have to learn to dance with salsa!

I continue to find myself when I dig into God's Word each day. And when I pray for each of my four children and my grandchildren, I am reminded of the truth that my birth daughter Sarah felt the Lord say to her. "Do you think you can do a better job loving them than I can? You think you love them more than I do? Let them go and trust that I have a better plan."

As I look back on my role as a mother, just like Hannah I can say, "My heart rejoices in the Lord." Our heavenly Father is not cruel. He is full of heart-stopping kindness. He does not forget us. His holy love is so great, we are engraved on the palms of his hands.

The Mother of My Child

I never ever knew your name.
I never knew from whence you came,
but gazing down at the sleeping child
I thought of you and I ached inside.
I bore you up before our God.
The sacrifice had been so hard.
One day somehow, somewhere, some place,
would God allow you to see her face?
I loved her, I cared for her, she was my own,
we laughed, we cried, she brought joy to our home.
I watched her skate, I heard her sing,
my heart was glad as she served the King.
Mother of my child, you were always in my heart,
I thought of you, I prayed for you, in my life you had a part.

Your eyes, your nose, the color of your hair,
your height, your walk, what all did she share?
The spring morning dawned, the sun shone bright,
today I would meet you—it seemed so right.
God had intervened in an unbelievable way,
only He could have planned this miraculous day.
And now together we can join hands,
as she and her husband go to far distant lands,
prayed for much more than so many others,
'Cos God had planned she would have
TWO MOTHERS

~ Sheila Callanan

Acknowledgments

Finding Sarah, Finding Me is a dream come true. Throughout this 230-page narrative I have endeavored to thank my precious God for this love story that encompasses so much with the various adoptions and reunions, and so many people. But this love story could never have been written if it were not for my beloved husband, David, whom I have stated before and will repeat here again, is the template for all my fictional heroes. I think the past 230 pages have shown fully how much I love and admire each of my children and grandchildren. So now a few of my dear friends deserve some of the limelight.

Thank you Rachel Phifer, not only for being my dear critique partner in all I write, but the gifted and award-winning author of the novel *The Language of Sparrows*. You have been my right arm in this non-fiction book. All the shining literary parts came from you, I'm sure.

My love and thanks goes to my publisher and editor Roseanna White of WhiteFire Publishing, whose final editing has polished this story to a gem worthy of her own award-winning skills as an author. And Wendy Chorot, my editor throughout the process from manuscript proposal to published book, my love and thanks from the bottom of my heart. You two were the literary rocks I could rest upon.

As for the rest of my friends throughout this journey; how can I possibly list all of you who cried with me, laughed with me, encouraged me? But I must mention a very few: Eric and Kathryn, thank you for so much—being there for David and me, and taking the photos of my two beautiful daughters for the front covers of my first two novels.

My heart-felt thanks to Dr. Garry Grams, now retired from your position as Behavioral Medicine Specialist and Family Therapist in the Faculty of Medicine at the University of British Columbia, for your wonderful counselling help. And Bob and Beverly Trainor for your sweet and integral part in this family story.

And to my many, many brothers and sisters at Sardis Fellowship Baptist Church; all I can do is roll my thanks to all of you into one big ball of appreciation as I address it to David and Emily Lee our pastor and his wife. Thank you all for your constant encouragement. And the same to my old friends at Burnett Baptist Church in Maple Ridge.

Lastly, a special thanks to my cat Scottie for always keeping my feet warm while I write. And to my readers—how much I appreciate each of you and the love you send back to me. Keep in touch with me through my author website and newsletter on www.ChristineLindsay.org.

Christine Lindsay's Fiction Titles from WhiteFire Publishing

Shadowed in Silk

~ Twilight of the British Raj ~
Book 1

Captured by Moonlight

~ Twilight of the British Raj ~
Book 2

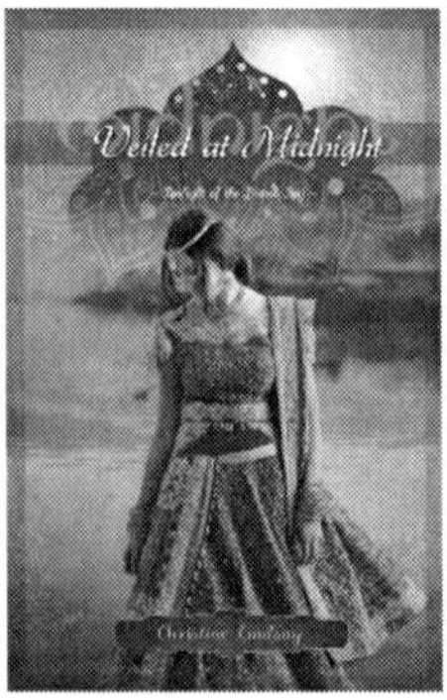

Veiled at Midnight

~ Twilight of the British Raj ~
Book 3

Don't miss these other titles from WhiteFire Publishing

Stone by Stone: Tear Down the Wall Between God's Heart and Yours
by Jasona Brown

With Stone by Stone Jasona will help you identify and remove ten stones possibly obstructing your intimacy with God—including guilt, unforgiveness, lies, and unhealed memories—so you can delight in the joy of knowing God's love for you as his beloved son or daughter.

Broken Umbrellas
by Emma Broch Stuart

We are all surrounded by brokenness, around us and inside us—from divorce, from abuse, from loss. We try to relate and serve, to love and protect...but how can we, when we ourselves our broken? In this transparent and honest look into humanity's deepest hurts, hope for our relationships comes through the ultimate Relationship with the Lord.

No Plan B: Discover God's Blueprint for Your Life
by Nelson Hannah

God has one plan for you. He created all of us to enjoy Plan A: a relationship with God, an identity from God, and a purpose in God. It's time for Christians to reject the lie of a Plan B...and embrace God's true design for our lives.

CPSIA information can be obtained at www.ICGtesting.com
Printed in the USA
LVOW07s0737070916

503522LV00002BA/7/P